On
Entrepreneurship
and Startups

HBR's 10 Must Reads series is the definitive collection of ideas and best practices for aspiring and experienced leaders alike. These books offer essential reading selected from the pages of *Harvard Business Review* on topics critical to the success of every manager.

Titles include:

On
Entrepreneurship and Startups

HARVARD BUSINESS REVIEW PRESS
Boston, Massachusetts

Copyright 2018 Harvard Business School Publishing Corporation
All rights reserved
Printed in the United States of America
10 9 8 7 6 5 4 3 2 1

No part of this publication may be reproduced, stored in or introduced into a retrieval system, or transmitted, in any form, or by any means (electronic, mechanical, photocopying, recording, or otherwise), without the prior permission of the publisher. Requests for permission should be directed to permissions@hbsp.harvard.edu, or mailed to Permissions, Harvard Business School Publishing, 60 Harvard Way, Boston, Massachusetts 02163.

The web addresses referenced in this book were live and correct at the time of the book's publication but may be subject to change.

Library of Congress cataloging-in-publication information is forthcoming.

ISBN: 978-1-63369-438-5
eISBN: 978-1-63369-439-2

The paper used in this publication meets the requirements of the American National Standard for Permanence of Paper for Publications and Documents in Libraries and Archives Z39.48 1992.

Contents

On
Entrepreneurship
and Startups

Hiring an Entrepreneurial Leader

by Timothy Butler

ENTREPRENEURS HAVE BECOME THE NEW heroes of the business world. In the same way that Robert McNamara and his fellow Ford Motor Company "Whiz Kids" elevated general managers to star status, figures like Mark Zuckerberg and Steve Jobs have made entrepreneurs the latest business icons. At Harvard Business School, where I advise the career development program, even students who plan to join blue chip firms and have no intention of ever launching start-ups would be insulted if someone told them they weren't "entrepreneurial." I understand why: Entrepreneurialism is highly valued in today's labor market. Companies of all shapes and sizes aspire to be seen as highly innovative, nimble, and agile—all qualities traditionally ascribed to entrepreneurs.

Yet in their recruiting efforts, companies do not have a scientific way of separating true entrepreneurs from other talented candidates. Instead, they fall back on broad stereotypes.

In my research I've explored how firms can address that problem. In an effort to understand what makes entrepreneurs special, I've compared the psychological-testing results of more than 4,000 successful entrepreneurs from multiple countries against those of some 1,800 business leaders who described themselves as general managers but not as entrepreneurs. Unsurprisingly, the two groups had much in common. On 28 of 41 dimensions of leadership, there was little or no difference between their skills. Yet when I looked more closely, combining their skill assessments with data on their life interests and personality traits, I discovered that entrepreneurs had three distinguishing characteristics: *the ability to thrive in uncertainty, a passionate desire to author and own projects,* and unique *skill at persuasion.* I also found that many of the traits commonly associated with entrepreneurial leaders didn't truly apply.

For instance, entrepreneurs aren't always exceptionally creative. But they are more curious and restless. They aren't risk seekers—but they find uncertainty and novelty motivating. In this article I'll tackle some of the myths about entrepreneurs and explain the more nuanced reality. I'll also offer evidence-based, practical advice on interview questions and résumé screening that hiring managers can use to distinguish entrepreneurial candidates from other high-potential talent.

Know Your Requirements

Before looking to hire entrepreneurial leaders, managers must answer an important question: Does the company really need one? Not all organizational challenges call for an entrepreneurial approach. In my research successful founders as a group scored extremely high on a scale that measures the desire for power and control—and notably higher than the nonentrepreneurial leaders. This quality can cause conflict in situations where the sharing of information and power is vital to organizational performance. What's more, it will often not play well in organizations that have established matrix structures, need porous boundaries between working groups, or require high levels of collaboration.

Hiring managers should carefully consider the particular leadership challenge they're recruiting for. If it's a greenfield situation, a turnaround, or any other circumstance that demands intensive initiative on a contained project, then an entrepreneurial style is likely to add value. But if the situation involves a highly interdependent matrix of working units, you might well do better looking for a different leadership profile.

Idea in Brief

The Problem

Though entrepreneurs are the new heroes of the business world, most companies lack a scientific approach to recruiting managers with entrepreneurial qualities. Instead, they rely on stereotypes.

The Solution

An analysis of the psychological-testing results of more than 4,000 entrepreneurs and 1,800 general managers showed that three factors differenti-

ate entrepreneurs: thriving in uncertainty, passion for ownership, and skill at persuasion.

The Upshot

Entrepreneurs aren't always more creative than general managers, but they enjoy pushing boundaries. They aren't risk seekers but find novelty motivating. Much like artists, they want to author and own projects. And they're natural salespeople. Hiring managers should look for these qualities when recruiting.

If you do conclude that an entrepreneurial leader is what your organization needs, then it's important to understand the entrepreneurial character in a nuanced, sophisticated way. Let's take a look now at the popular perceptions about entrepreneurship and at what the research indicates really drives the people who are good at it.

The stereotype: Entrepreneurs are unusually creative.
The subtler truth: Entrepreneurs are curious seekers of adventure, learning, and opportunity.

One popular notion is that entrepreneurs and people who enjoy constantly changing, innovative environments are more creative than others. But there are many types of creativity in business. Some managers, for instance, are highly creative at fixing things that are broken and enjoy the challenge of returning a system to a previous state of optimal functioning. While it's certainly true that entrepreneurs excel at original thinking, so do many nonentrepreneurs. In reality, what sets entrepreneurial individuals apart is something slightly different— something both broader and deeper than what is typically evoked by the word "creativity." It's the ability to thrive in uncertainty.

A critical aspect to this dimension is *openness to new experiences*. In my research, I've found that it is the single trait that most distinguishes leaders who are entrepreneurial from their more conventional peers.

Openness to new experiences is about having a restless need to explore and learn. It entails not just a willingness to proceed in unpredictable environments but a heightened state of motivation that occurs at the edge of the unknown and the untried. For individuals who score high on this dimension, the unknown is a source of excitement rather than anxiety.

Consider Charlotte Yates, who brought her entrepreneurial leadership style to Sprint and IBM before eventually leaving to help found the telecommunications firm Telwares. When she was in a larger corporate setting, she saw herself as taking an approach that differed from the one used by the majority of her fellow leaders. "I didn't follow IBM's design process and their normal chain of command, because my task would have never gotten done," she says. "I didn't see myself as having a tightly defined box; I didn't see the boundaries. I was looking at a blank piece of paper and saying to myself, 'Now, what do I want to create here?'"

Entrepreneurs enjoy the "dreaming it up" process. Like Yates, they are less bound by convention than their corporate counterparts, and they're more likely to assume things can be done better. For this reason, they thrive in environments where there is a market opportunity but no product or service, or where there is a product but the go-to-market strategy is not clear. They relish the early stages of projects and tend to become less engaged as projects become more routinized and steady state.

The stereotype: Entrepreneurs enjoy and seek risk.
The subtler truth: Entrepreneurs are more comfortable with risk.

Another prevailing view is that entrepreneurial people love risk— that they enjoy the thrill of taking chances. This is not true; entrepreneurs are not the skydivers of the business world. Like every good businessperson, they seek to minimize risk at every opportunity. However, many studies have shown that entrepreneurs have higher comfort with risk than conventional managers. In other words, when accepting risk is necessary to reach a desired goal, entrepreneurs are better at living with it and managing the anxiety that might be disabling to others. My research likewise showed that the colleagues of entrepreneurial leaders rated them significantly higher than more-traditional executives on comfort with risk.

Entrepreneurial leaders aren't necessarily tougher and more stress-hardy than their corporate peers—in ratings of their resiliency, taken from 360 reviews, I found no significant difference between the two groups. Rather, the point that emerged was that highly unpredictable and ambiguous environments are, for entrepreneurial leaders, a source of motivation. This is a second reason they thrive in uncertainty.

Assessing the ability to thrive in uncertainty

Openness to new experiences and comfort with risk are the main components of the ability to perform well in unpredictable environments, although many people misperceive the essentials to be tough-mindedness, hardiness, or resilience. Those are highly desirable qualities in a leader (and your organization's situation may demand them), but they're beside the point if your hunt is for an entrepreneurial leader.

Here's what to examine instead: Has the candidate made choices that clearly favor adventure and learning over convention and minimization of risk? Examples might include choosing a less recognized college to pursue a particular passion; spending a year abroad in an unusual setting as a growth experience; opting to work for a highly innovative small company rather than a big brand-name company; vacation destinations that involve hardship but unusual experiences; living in a diverse and interesting part of a city rather than the usual professional enclaves; taking genuine risks in previous organizational roles; and taking on projects for which resources are scarce and outcomes uncertain.

When interviewed, entrepreneurial managers will ask bold questions, take the initiative in the conversation, exhibit little anxiety about fitting in or providing the desired responses, and exude sheer, almost impatient, enthusiasm. Do candidates' answers feel safe or "rule-bound"? Don't miss any opportunity that allows candidates to demonstrate their willingness and capacity to explore the unknown.

The following questions will help you identify candidates who will thrive in uncertainty. But don't look for the best answers; look for the extent to which the candidate champions the value of exploration, learning, new approaches, and willingness to take on risk to achieve an important outcome.

- Which do you fear most: anxiety or frustration?

- Are you willing to get into trouble in order to make something important happen?

- Which is more valuable: instinct or wisdom? Why?

- Which is more valuable: imagination or analysis? Why?

- A space explorer is looking for people to colonize Mars. Have a conversation between the part of you that would say yes to this mission and the part that would say no.

- We (or a competitor) decided to launch this product in this way. How could we have done it differently?

- Rapidly, choose one option from each of the following word pairs. (Do not try to score these responses, but look for a general pattern.)

  consistency or **flexibility**
  proven or **potential**
  careful or **bold**
  explore or **settle**
  predictable or **possible**
  bonus or **salary**
  safety or **opportunity**

medal or joy
puzzle or blank canvas
nimble or steady
change or constant
known or unknown
patience or excitement
frontier or home
set or open
wild or tame
variety or certainty
inherit or create

The stereotype: Entrepreneurs are more personally ambitious than other leaders.
The subtler truth: Entrepreneurs are driven by a need to own products, projects, and initiatives.

As mentioned earlier, entrepreneurial leaders, as a group, score exceptionally high on the need for power and control, and notably higher than conventional general managers (though that group scores quite high too). Intrigued by this, I interviewed entrepreneurs to learn more. I began to discern an interesting variation on the need for power often associated with entrepreneurial leaders: For them, it's less about dominance and more about ownership. It's not about having supremacy over subordinates or commanding respect or authority; it's about having control over the finished product. In this way, entrepreneurs have more in common with authors and artists than with dictators.

Entrepreneurial managers are hands-on. They want to be in the middle of the buzz and hustle as a new venture, day by day, comes into the world and starts to walk, then run. They are not ones to sit in tastefully appointed corner offices moving chess pieces for a game being played out floors below them. They want to be the artisans with their hands on the wet clay. They want to take a finished piece from the kiln and say, "This is mine"—not in an egotistical or acquisitive sense but in the sense of "I shape materials that become valuable and useful things." Long after Apple had become one of the largest companies in history, Steve Jobs still had to be part of every critical design discussion, hold prototypes in his hand, and assess every detail from gleam to heft. Power, for the entrepreneurial spirit, is about being the owner of and driving force behind an initiative.

One entrepreneurial leader I interviewed, Andrea Kimmel, CEO of Sweet Kiddles, a childcare start-up, put it this way: "I want people to see me as the person who can make ideas happen. For me, part of being the boss means that people in the organization will come to me to try to make things happen, to bring change."

This expression of power is different from positional power (which is based on your rank), charismatic power (influencing people through your personality), or expert power (when others defer to your knowledge). Entrepreneurial leaders do not see themselves as exerting power from above. They see their role as being at the center of a circle rather than the top of a pyramid. An entrepreneur may or may not be charismatic, but his method is not to inspire the masses at the annual convention and then step off the stage and retreat to the corner office. He wants to have a hand in the immediate game.

That is not to say that entrepreneurial leaders do not display aspects of authority, expertise, or charisma—many do. But the aspect that unites them is not the desire to be a decision maker. For such leaders, a venture is an expression to the world of who they are.

Assessing passion for ownership
To find out who has a hunger for hands-on involvement in projects, from start to finish, try to tease out the following: Has the candidate been a founder rather than a joiner? Instead of running for class office, for instance, did she start a new club, campus initiative, or business? (Points should be awarded for a pattern of seeking out leadership of any kind, however.) Did she make early career choices that would give her creative control? Has her path been atypical or opportunistic rather than one of lockstep promotions? Has she been "in charge of her life" from an early age? Has she been an entrepreneur, successful or not, at any stage?

Then watch for these signs: Does the candidate "own" the interview by starting to sketch out a vision for how the demands of the position could be met? Does she (ideally without arrogance) participate almost right away as a mutual "owner" of any problem at hand? Does she probe for assurances that she will have the requisite autonomy to lead the new venture?

Some interview questions to consider:

- Which business leaders do you admire? Why?

- What do you take pride in?

- What causes new ventures to fail more often: a lack of leadership or a lack of collaboration?

- Which is a better attitude for a business leader: passion or professionalism?

- Psychologically, do you take work home with you?

- How much of who you are is what you do at work?

- Rapidly, choose one option from each of the following word pairs. (Again, do not try to score these responses, but look for a general pattern.)

  > **own** or **manage**
  > **suggest** or **direct**
  > **lead** or **participate**
  > **shape** or **control**
  > **captain** or **navigator**
  > **ownership** or **title**
  > **grace** or **power**
  > **complete** or **reflect**
  > **aspire** or **accomplish**
  > **membership** or **possession**
  > **knowledge** or **power**
  > **president** or **minister**
  > **profit** or **equity**

The stereotype: Entrepreneurs are natural salespeople.
The truth: This one is correct.

My research corroborated many earlier studies that highlighted the importance of confidence and persuasiveness among entrepreneurial leaders. When it's crucial to get somewhere or make something happen, but it's not clear how to do so, you must, first, believe that you can reach your goal and, second, convince all the people whose help you need that you can, too—and very often, with little or no evidence to back you up.

Entrepreneurs must be able to sell their vision to prospective team members before they have anything else to offer. Many have to sell their ideas to initial investors and later to venture capitalists and joint-venture partners. And all entrepreneurs must be able to sell to the customer.

The same applies to people spearheading new ventures within larger corporate entities. The renowned U.S. automobile executive Lee Iacocca was an entrepreneurial leader who spent his entire career in large corporate settings. Though he'd been trained as an engineer, he switched to a sales track early on, and it was his sales ability that made him exceptional. His persuasive skill helped him at every turn. Two of his sales feats assumed mythic status: Convincing Ford's leadership that the firm should make a large investment in the development of a lower-priced sports car (which led to the phenomenal Mustang success story) and getting Congress to pass an unprecedented act bailing out Chrysler.

Assessing persuasiveness

Evaluating persuasiveness is different from evaluating the ability to thrive in uncertainty and the passion for ownership. Most of the evidence will come directly from interactions with candidates. Leaders high on this dimension will exude confidence and genuinely convince you that they can get the job done. Their confidence won't feel like bluster or hype but will seem well-founded. They'll probe the relevant issues and potential courses of action in a steady and intelligent way.

They will be honest about the unknowns of the situation but, at the same time, not waver about their ability to overcome contingencies.

Here are some interview questions about past behavior that may be helpful, although the answers should be weighted less than a candidate's actual behavior and attitudes during the selection process. Essentially, you should assess this entrepreneurial leadership dimension as if you were hiring for an executive sales position.

- What experience have you had with sales?

- Could you tell me about a particularly challenging sales experience you've had?

- Could you describe a life situation when it was extremely important that you change the opinion of others?

- How does persuading a group of executive peers differ from selling to a customer?

Exceptional leaders have much in common, and most can adapt to the demands of whatever organizational challenges they face. Leaders who are truly entrepreneurial, however, excel when a situation demands complete ownership of a venture or problem, become more motivated as uncertainty increases, and have a remarkable ability to persuade others to follow their course of action. This profile can be problematic in complex organizations where established business units need to work intensely together, across boundaries, and leaders need to share both information and power on a daily basis. But if your organization needs someone to turn innovative ideas into full-blown, standalone enterprises—or invent and bring to life completely new models—it may be time to hire an entrepreneurial leader. And by following the advice in this article, you can make sure you actually find what you're looking for.

Originally published in March–April 2017. Reprint R1702E

How to Write a Great Business Plan

by William A. Sahlman

FEW AREAS OF BUSINESS ATTRACT as much attention as new ventures, and few aspects of new-venture creation attract as much attention as the business plan. Countless books and articles in the popular press dissect the topic. A growing number of annual business-plan contests are springing up across the United States and, increasingly, in other countries. Both graduate and undergraduate schools devote entire courses to the subject. Indeed, judging by all the hoopla surrounding business plans, you would think that the only things standing between a would-be entrepreneur and spectacular success are glossy five-color charts, a bundle of meticulous-looking spreadsheets, and a decade of month-by-month financial projections.

Nothing could be further from the truth. In my experience with hundreds of entrepreneurial startups, business plans rank no higher than 2—on a scale from 1 to 10—as a predictor of a new venture's success. And sometimes, in fact, the more elaborately crafted the document, the more likely the venture is to, well, flop, for lack of a more euphemistic word.

What's wrong with most business plans? The answer is relatively straightforward. Most waste too much ink on numbers and devote too little to the information that really matters to intelligent investors. As every seasoned investor knows, financial projections for a new company—especially detailed, month-by-month projections that stretch out for more than a year—are an act of imagination. An entrepreneurial venture faces far too many unknowns to predict revenues, let alone profits. Moreover, few if any entrepreneurs correctly anticipate how much capital and time will be required to accomplish their objectives. Typically, they are wildly optimistic, padding their projections. Investors know about the padding effect and therefore discount the figures in business plans. These maneuvers create a vicious circle of inaccuracy that benefits no one.

Don't misunderstand me: business plans should include some numbers. But those numbers should appear mainly in the form of a business model that shows the entrepreneurial team has thought through the key drivers of the venture's success or failure. In manufacturing, such a driver might be the yield on a production process; in magazine publishing, the anticipated renewal rate; or in software, the impact of using various distribution channels. The model should also address the break-even issue: At what level of sales does the business begin to make a profit? And even more important, When does cash flow turn positive? Without a doubt, these questions deserve a few pages in any business plan. Near the back.

What goes at the front? What information does a good business plan contain?

If you want to speak the language of investors—and also make sure you have asked yourself the right questions before setting out on the most daunting journey of a businessperson's career—I recommend basing your business plan on the framework that follows. It does not provide the kind of "winning" formula touted by some current how-to books and software programs for entrepreneurs. Nor is it a guide to brain surgery. Rather, the framework systematically assesses the four interdependent factors critical to every new venture:

> **The People.** The men and women starting and running the venture, as well as the outside parties providing key services or important resources for it, such as its lawyers, accountants, and suppliers.

> **The Opportunity.** A profile of the business itself—what it will sell and to whom, whether the business can grow and how fast, what its economics are, who and what stand in the way of success.

Idea in Brief

Every seasoned investor knows that detailed financial projections for a new company are an act of imagination. Nevertheless, most business plans pour far too much ink on the numbers—and far too little on the information that really matters. Why? William Sahlman suggests that a great business plan is one that focuses on a series of questions. These questions relate to the four factors critical to the success of every new venture: the people, the opportunity, the context, and the possibilities for both risk and reward.

The questions about people revolve around three issues: What do they know? Whom do they know? And, How well are they known? As for opportunity, the plan should focus on two questions: Is the market for the venture's product or service large or rapidly growing (or preferably both)? and Is the industry structurally attractive? Then, in addition to demonstrating an understanding of the context in which their venture will operate, entrepreneurs should make clear how they will respond when that context inevitably changes. Finally, the plan should look unflinchingly at the risks the new venture faces, giving would-be backers a realistic idea of what magnitude of reward they can expect and when they can expect it.

A great business plan is not easy to compose, Sahlman acknowledges, largely because most entrepreneurs are wild-eyed optimists. But one that asks the right questions is a powerful tool. A better deal, not to mention a better shot at success, awaits entrepreneurs who use it.

The Context. The big picture—the regulatory environment, interest rates, demographic trends, inflation, and the like— basically, factors that inevitably change but cannot be controlled by the entrepreneur.

Risk and Reward. An assessment of everything that can go wrong and right, and a discussion of how the entrepreneurial team can respond.

The assumption behind the framework is that great businesses have attributes that are easy to identify but hard to assemble. They have an experienced, energetic managerial team from the top to the bottom. The team's members have skills and experiences directly relevant to the opportunity they are pursuing. Ideally, they will have

Business Plans: For Entrepreneurs Only?

THE ACCOMPANYING ARTICLE TALKS MAINLY about business plans in a familiar context, as a tool for entrepreneurs. But quite often, start-ups are launched within established companies. Do those new ventures require business plans? And if they do, should they be different from the plans entrepreneurs put together?

The answer to the first question is an emphatic yes; the answer to the second, an equally emphatic no. All new ventures—whether they are funded by venture capitalists or, as is the case with intrapreneurial businesses, by shareholders—need to pass the same acid tests. After all, the marketplace does not differentiate between products or services based on who is pouring money into them behind the scenes.

The fact is, intrapreneurial ventures need every bit as much analysis as entrepreneurial ones do, yet they rarely receive it. Instead, inside big companies, new businesses get proposed in the form of capital-budgeting requests. These faceless documents are subject to detailed financial scrutiny and a consensus-building process, as the project wends its way through the chain of command, what I call the "neutron bomb" model of project governance. However, in the history of such proposals, a plan never has been submitted that did not promise returns in excess of corporate hurdle rates. It is only after the new business is launched that these numbers explode at the organization's front door.

That problem could be avoided in large part if intrapreneurial ventures followed the guidelines set out in the accompanying article. For instance, busi-

worked successfully together in the past. The opportunity has an attractive, sustainable business model; it is possible to create a competitive edge and defend it. Many options exist for expanding the scale and scope of the business, and these options are unique to the enterprise and its team. Value can be extracted from the business in a number of ways either through a positive harvest event— a sale—or by scaling down or liquidating. The context is favorable with respect to both the regulatory and the macro-economic environments. Risk is understood, and the team has considered ways to mitigate the impact of difficult events. In short, great businesses have the four parts of the framework completely covered. If only reality were so neat.

ness plans for such a venture should begin with the résumés of all the people involved. What has the team done in the past that would suggest it would be successful in the future, and so on? In addition, the new venture's product or service should be fully analyzed in terms of its opportunity and context. Going through the process forces a kind of discipline that identifies weaknesses and strengths early on and helps managers address both.

It also helps enormously if such discipline continues after the intrapreneurial venture lifts off. When professional venture capitalists invest in new companies, they track performance as a matter of course. But in large companies, scrutiny of a new venture is often inconsistent. That shouldn't or needn't be the case. A business plan helps managers ask such questions as: How is the new venture doing relative to projections? What decisions has the team made in response to new information? Have changes in the context made additional funding necessary? How could the team have predicted those changes? Such questions not only keep a new venture running smoothly but also help an organization learn from its mistakes and triumphs.

Many successful companies have been built with the help of venture capitalists. Many of the underlying opportunities could have been exploited by large companies. Why weren't they? Perhaps useful lessons can be learned by studying the world of independent ventures, one lesson being: Write a great business plan.

The People

When I receive a business plan, I always read the résumé section first. Not because the people part of the new venture is the most important, but because without the right team, none of the other parts really matters.

I read the résumés of the venture's team with a list of questions in mind. (See the sidebar "Who Are These People, Anyway?") All these questions get at the same three issues about the venture's team members: What do they know? Whom do they know? and How well are they known?

What and whom they know are matters of insight and experience. How familiar are the team members with industry players and

Who Are These People, Anyway?

Fourteen "Personal" Questions Every Business Plan Should Answer

- Where are the founders from?
- Where have they been educated?
- Where have they worked—and for whom?
- What have they accomplished—professionally and personally—in the past?
- What is their reputation within the business community?
- What experience do they have that is directly relevant to the opportunity they are pursuing?
- What skills, abilities, and knowledge do they have?
- How realistic are they about the venture's chances for success and the tribulations it will face?
- Who else needs to be on the team?
- Are they prepared to recruit high-quality people?
- How will they respond to adversity?
- Do they have the mettle to make the inevitable hard choices that have to be made?
- How committed are they to this venture?
- What are their motivations?

dynamics? Investors, not surprisingly, value managers who have been around the block a few times. A business plan should candidly describe each team member's knowledge of the new venture's type of product or service; its production processes; and the market itself, from competitors to customers. It also helps to indicate whether the team members have worked together before. Not played—as in roomed together in college—but *worked*.

Investors also look favorably on a team that is known because the real world often prefers not to deal with start-ups. They're too unpredictable. That changes, however, when the new company is run by people well known to suppliers, customers, and employees.

Their enterprise may be brand new, but they aren't. The surprise element of working with a start-up is somewhat ameliorated.

Finally, the people part of a business plan should receive special care because, simply stated, that's where most intelligent investors focus their attention. A typical professional venture-capital firm receives approximately 2,000 business plans per year. These plans are filled with tantalizing ideas for new products and services that will change the world and reap billions in the process—or so they say. But the fact is, most venture capitalists believe that ideas are a dime a dozen: only execution skills count. As Arthur Rock, a venture capital legend associated with the formation of such companies as Apple, Intel, and Teledyne, states, "I invest in people, not ideas." Rock also has said, "If you can find good people, if they're wrong about the product, they'll make a switch, so what good is it to understand the product that they're talking about in the first place?"

Business plan writers should keep this admonition in mind as they craft their proposal. Talk about the people—exhaustively. And if there is nothing solid about their experience and abilities to herald, then the entrepreneurial team should think again about launching the venture.

The Opportunity

When it comes to the opportunity itself, a good business plan begins by focusing on two questions: Is the total market for the venture's product or service large, rapidly growing, or both? Is the industry now, or can it become, structurally attractive? Entrepreneurs and investors look for large or rapidly growing markets mainly because it is often easier to obtain a share of a growing market than to fight with entrenched competitors for a share of a mature or stagnant market. Smart investors, in fact, try hard to identify high-growth-potential markets early in their evolution: that's where the big payoffs are. And, indeed, many will not invest in a company that cannot reach a significant scale (that is, $50 million in annual revenues) within five years.

As for attractiveness, investors are obviously looking for markets that actually allow businesses to make some money. But that's not the no-brainer it seems. In the late 1970s, the computer disk-drive business looked very attractive. The technology was new and exciting. Dozens of companies jumped into the fray, aided by an army of professional investors. Twenty years later, however, the thrill is gone for managers and investors alike. Disk drive companies must design products to meet the perceived needs of original equipment manufacturers (OEMs) and end users. Selling a product to OEMs is complicated. The customers are large relative to most of their suppliers. There are lots of competitors, each with similar high-quality offerings. Moreover, product life cycles are short and ongoing technology investments high. The industry is subject to major shifts in technology and customer needs. Intense rivalry leads to lower prices and, hence, lower margins. In short, the disk drive industry is simply not set up to make people a lot of money; it's a structural disaster area.

The information services industry, by contrast, is paradise. Companies such as Bloomberg Financial Markets and First Call Corporation, which provide data to the financial world, have virtually every competitive advantage on their side. First, they can assemble or create *proprietary* content—content that, by the way, is like life's blood to thousands of money managers and stock analysts around the world. And although it is often expensive to develop the service and to acquire initial customers, once up and running, these companies can deliver content to customers very cheaply. Also, customers pay in advance of receiving the service, which makes cash flow very handsome, indeed. In short, the structure of the information services industry is beyond attractive: it's gorgeous. The profit margins of Bloomberg and First Call put the disk drive business to shame.

Thus, the first step for entrepreneurs is to make sure they are entering an industry that is large and/or growing, and one that's structurally attractive. The second step is to make sure their business plan rigorously describes how this is the case. And if it isn't the case, their business plan needs to specify how the venture will still manage to make enough of a profit that investors (or potential employees or suppliers, for that matter) will want to participate.

The Opportunity of a Lifetime—or Is It?

Nine Questions About the Business Every Business Plan Should Answer

- Who is the new venture's customer?
- How does the customer make decisions about buying this product or service?
- To what degree is the product or service a compelling purchase for the customer?
- How will the product or service be priced?
- How will the venture reach all the identified customer segments?
- How much does it cost (in time and resources) to acquire a customer?
- How much does it cost to produce and deliver the product or service?
- How much does it cost to support a customer?
- How easy is it to retain a customer?

Once it examines the new venture's industry, a business plan must describe in detail how the company will build and launch its product or service into the marketplace. Again, a series of questions should guide the discussion. (See the sidebar "The Opportunity of a Lifetime—or Is It?")

Often the answers to these questions reveal a fatal flaw in the business. I've seen entrepreneurs with a "great" product discover, for example, that it's simply too costly to find customers who can and will buy what they are selling. Economically viable access to customers is the key to business, yet many entrepreneurs take the *Field of Dreams* approach to this notion: build it, and they will come. That strategy works in the movies but is not very sensible in the real world.

It is not always easy to answer questions about the likely consumer response to new products or services. The market is as fickle as it is unpredictable. (Who would have guessed that plug-in room deodorizers would sell?) One entrepreneur I know proposed to introduce an electronic news-clipping service. He made his pitch to a prospective venture-capital investor who rejected the plan, stating,

"I just don't think the dogs will eat the dog food." Later, when the entrepreneur's company went public, he sent the venture capitalist an anonymous package containing an empty can of dog food and a copy of his prospectus. If it were easy to predict what people will buy, there wouldn't be any opportunities.

Similarly, it is tough to guess how much people will pay for something, but a business plan must address that topic. Sometimes, the dogs will eat the dog food, but only at a price less than cost. Investors always look for opportunities for value pricing—that is, markets in which the costs to produce the product are low, but consumers will still pay a lot for it. No one is dying to invest in a company when margins are skinny. Still, there is money to be made in inexpensive products and services—even in commodities. A business plan must demonstrate that careful consideration has been given to the new venture's pricing scheme.

The list of questions about the new venture's opportunity focuses on the direct revenues and the costs of producing and marketing a product. That's fine, as far as it goes. A sensible proposal, however, also involves assessing the business model from a perspective that takes into account the investment required—that is, the balance sheet side of the equation. The following questions should also be addressed so that investors can understand the cash flow implications of pursuing an opportunity:

- When does the business have to buy resources, such as supplies, raw materials, and people?

- When does the business have to pay for them?

- How long does it take to acquire a customer?

- How long before the customer sends the business a check?

- How much capital equipment is required to support a dollar of sales?

Investors, of course, are looking for businesses in which management can buy low, sell high, collect early, and pay late. The business plan needs to spell out how close to that ideal the new venture is expected to come. Even if the answer is "not very"—and it usually is—at least the truth is out there to discuss.

The opportunity section of a business plan must also bring a few other issues to the surface. First, it must demonstrate and analyze how an opportunity can grow—in other words, how the new venture can expand its range of products or services, customer base, or geographic scope. Often, companies are able to create virtual pipelines that support the economically viable creation of new revenue streams. In the publishing business, for example, *Inc.* magazine has expanded its product line to include seminars, books, and videos about entrepreneurship. Similarly, building on the success of its personal-finance software program Quicken, Intuit now sells software for electronic banking, small-business accounting, and tax preparation, as well as personal-printing supplies and on-line information services—to name just a few of its highly profitable ancillary spin-offs.

Now, lots of business plans runneth over on the subject of the new venture's potential for growth and expansion. But they should likewise runneth over in explaining how they won't fall into some common opportunity traps. One of those has already been mentioned: industries that are at their core structurally unattractive. But there are others. The world of invention, for example, is fraught with danger. Over the past 15 years, I have seen scores of individuals who have devised a better mousetrap—newfangled creations from inflatable pillows for use on airplanes to automated car-parking systems. Few of these idea-driven companies have really taken off, however. I'm not entirely sure why. Sometimes, the inventor refuses to spend the money required by or share the rewards sufficiently with the business side of the company. Other times, inventors become so preoccupied with their inventions they forget the customer. Whatever the reason, better-mousetrap businesses have an uncanny way of malfunctioning.

Another opportunity trap that business plans—and entrepreneurs in general—need to pay attention to is the tricky business of arbitrage. Basically, arbitrage ventures are created to take advantage of some pricing disparity in the marketplace. MCI Communications

Corporation, for instance, was formed to offer long-distance service at a lower price than AT&T. Some of the industry consolidations going on today reflect a different kind of arbitrage—the ability to buy small businesses at a wholesale price, roll them up together into a larger package, and take them public at a retail price, all without necessarily adding value in the process.

Taking advantage of arbitrage opportunities is a viable and potentially profitable way to enter a business. In the final analysis, however, all arbitrage opportunities evaporate. It is not a question of whether, only when. The trick in these businesses is to use the arbitrage profits to build a more enduring business model, and business plans must explain how and when that will occur.

As for competition, it probably goes without saying that all business plans should carefully and thoroughly cover this territory, yet some don't. That is a glaring omission. For starters, every business plan should answer the following questions about the competition:

- Who are the new venture's current competitors?

- What resources do they control? What are their strengths and weaknesses?

- How will they respond to the new venture's decision to enter the business?

- How can the new venture respond to its competitors' response?

- Who else might be able to observe and exploit the same opportunity?

- Are there ways to co-opt potential or actual competitors by forming alliances?

Business is like chess: to be successful, you must anticipate several moves in advance. A business plan that describes an insuperable lead or a proprietary market position is by definition written by naive people. That goes not just for the competition section of the business plan but for the entire discussion of the opportunity. All opportunities have promise; all have vulnerabilities. A good business plan doesn't whitewash the latter. Rather, it proves that the entrepreneurial team knows the good, the bad, and the ugly that the venture faces ahead.

The Context

Opportunities exist in a context. At one level is the macroeconomic environment, including the level of economic activity, inflation, exchange rates, and interest rates. At another level are the wide range of government rules and regulations that affect the opportunity and how resources are marshaled to exploit it. Examples extend from tax policy to the rules about raising capital for a private or public company. And at yet another level are factors like technology that define the limits of what a business or its competitors can accomplish.

Context often has a tremendous impact on every aspect of the entrepreneurial process, from identification of opportunity to harvest. In some cases, changes in some contextual factor create opportunity. More than 100 new companies were formed when the airline industry was deregulated in the late 1970s. The context for financing was also favorable, enabling new entrants like People Express to go to the public market for capital even before starting operations.

Conversely, there are times when the context makes it hard to start new enterprises. The recession of the early 1990s combined with a difficult financing environment for new companies: venture capital disbursements were low, as was the amount of capital raised in the public markets. (Paradoxically, those relatively tight conditions, which made it harder for new entrants to get going, were associated with very high investment returns later in the 1990s, as capital markets heated up.)

Sometimes, a shift in context turns an unattractive business into an attractive one, and vice versa. Consider the case of a packaging company some years ago that was performing so poorly it was about to be put on the block. Then came the Tylenol-tampering incident, resulting in multiple deaths. The packaging company happened to have an efficient mechanism for installing tamper-proof seals, and in a matter of weeks its financial performance could have been called spectacular. Conversely, U.S. tax reforms enacted in 1986 created havoc for companies in the real estate business, eliminating almost every positive incentive to invest. Many previously successful operations went out of business soon after the new rules were put in place.

Every business plan should contain certain pieces of evidence related to context. First, the entrepreneurs should show a heightened awareness of the new venture's context and how it helps or hinders their specific proposal. Second, and more important, they should demonstrate that they know the venture's context will inevitably change and describe how those changes might affect the business. Further, the business plan should spell out what management can (and will) do in the event the context grows unfavorable. Finally, the business plan should explain the ways (if any) in which management can affect context in a positive way. For example, management might be able to have an impact on regulations or on industry standards through lobbying efforts.

Risk and Reward

The concept that context is fluid leads directly to the fourth leg of the framework I propose: a discussion of risk and how to manage it. I've come to think of a good business plan as a snapshot of an event in the future. That's quite a feat to begin with—taking a picture of the unknown. But the best business plans go beyond that; they are like movies of the future. They show the people, the opportunity, and the context from multiple angles. They offer a plausible, coherent story of what lies ahead. They unfold possibilities of action and reaction.

Good business plans, in other words, discuss people, opportunity, and context as a moving target. All three factors (and the relationship among them) are likely to change over time as a company evolves from start-up to ongoing enterprise. Therefore, any business plan worth the time it takes to write or read needs to focus attention on the dynamic aspects of the entrepreneurial process.

Of course, the future is hard to predict. Still, it is possible to give potential investors a sense of the kind and class of risk and reward they are assuming with a new venture. All it takes is a pencil and two simple drawings. (See the sidebar "Visualizing Risk and Reward.") But even with these drawings, risk is, well, risky. In reality, there are no immutable distributions of outcomes. It is ultimately the responsibility of management to change the distribution, to increase the likelihood and consequences of success, and to decrease the likelihood and implications of problems.

One of the great myths about entrepreneurs is that they are risk seekers. All sane people want to avoid risk. As Harvard Business School professor (and venture capitalist) Howard Stevenson says, true entrepreneurs want to capture all the reward and give all the risk to others. The best business is a post office box to which people send cashier's checks. Yet risk is unavoidable. So what does that mean for a business plan?

It means that the plan must unflinchingly confront the risks ahead—in terms of people, opportunity, and context. What happens if one of the new venture's leaders leaves? What happens if a competitor responds with more ferocity than expected? What happens if there is a revolution in Namibia, the source of a key raw material? What will management actually *do*?

Those are hard questions for an entrepreneur to pose, especially when seeking capital. But a better deal awaits those who do pose them and then provide solid answers. A new venture, for example, might be highly leveraged and therefore very sensitive to interest rates. Its business plan would benefit enormously by stating that management intends to hedge its exposure through the financial-futures market by purchasing a contract that does well when interest rates go up. That is the equivalent of offering investors insurance. (It also makes sense for the business itself.)

Finally, one important area in the realm of risk/reward management relates to harvesting. Venture capitalists often ask if a company is "IPOable," by which they mean, Can the company be taken public at some point in the future? Some businesses are inherently difficult to take public because doing so would reveal information that might

Visualizing Risk and Reward

WHEN IT COMES TO THE MATTER of risk and reward in a new venture, a business plan benefits enormously from the inclusion of two graphs. Perhaps *graphs* is the wrong word; these are really just schematic pictures that illustrate the most likely relationship between risk and reward, that is, the relationship between the opportunity and its economics. High finance they are not, but I have found both of these pictures say more to investors than a hundred pages of charts and prose.

The first picture depicts the amount of money needed to launch the new venture, time to positive cash flow, and the expected magnitude of the payoff.

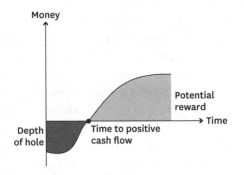

This image helps the investor understand the depth and duration of negative cash flow, as well as the relationship between the investment and the possible return. The ideal, needless to say, is to have cash flow early and often. But most investors are intrigued by the picture even when the cash outflow is high and long—as long as the cash inflow is more so.

Of course, since the world of new ventures is populated by wild-eyed optimists, you might expect the picture to display a shallower hole and a steeper reward slope than it should. It usually does. But to be honest, even that kind of picture belongs in the business plan because it is a fair warning to investors that the new venture's team is completely out of touch with reality and should be avoided at all costs.

---

harm its competitive position (for example, it would reveal profitability, thereby encouraging entry or angering customers or suppliers). Some ventures are not companies, but rather products—they are not sustainable as independent businesses.

Therefore, the business plan should talk candidly about the end of the process. How will the investor eventually get money out of

The second picture complements the first. It shows investors the range of possible returns and the likelihood of achieving them. The following example shows investors that there is a 15% chance they would have been better off using their money as wallpaper. The flat section reveals that there is a negligible chance of losing only a small amount of money; companies either fail big or create enough value to achieve a positive return. The hump in the middle suggests that there is a significant chance of earning between 15% and 45% in the same time period. And finally, there is a small chance that the initial outlay of cash will spawn a 200% internal rate of return, which might have occurred if you had happened to invest in Microsoft when it was a private company.

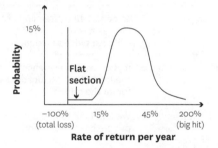

Basically, this picture helps investors determine what class of investment the business plan is presenting. Is the new venture drilling for North Sea oil—highly risky with potentially big payoffs—or is it digging development wells in Texas, which happens to be less of a geological gamble and probably less lucrative, too? This image answers that kind of question. It's then up to the investors to decide how much risk they want to live with against what kind of odds.

Again, the people who write business plans might be inclined to skew the picture to make it look as if the probability of a significant return is downright huge and the possibility of loss is negligible. And, again, I would say therein lies the picture's beauty. What it claims, checked against the investor's sense of reality and experience, should serve as a simple pictorial caveat emptor.

the business, assuming it is successful, even if only marginally so? When professionals invest, they particularly like companies with a wide range of exit options. They like companies that work hard to preserve and enhance those options along the way, companies that don't, for example, unthinkingly form alliances with big corporations that could someday actually *buy* them. Investors feel a

A Glossary of Business Plan Terms

What they say...	And what they really mean
We conservatively project . . .	We read a book that said we had to be a $50 million company in five years, and we reverse-engineered the numbers.
We took our best guess and divided by 2.	We accidentally divided by 0.5.
We project a 10% margin.	We did not modify any of the assumptions in the business plan template that we downloaded from the Internet.
The project is 98% complete.	To complete the remaining 2% will take as long as it took to create the initial 98% but will cost twice as much.
Our business model is proven . . .	if you take the evidence from the past week for the best of our 50 locations and extrapolate it for all the others.
We have a six-month lead.	We tried not to find out how many other people have a six-month lead.
We only need a 10% market share.	So do the other 50 entrants getting funded.
Customers are clamoring for our product.	We have not yet asked them to pay for it. Also, all of our current customers are relatives.
We are the low-cost producer.	We have not produced anything yet, but we are confident that we will be able to.
We have no competition.	Only IBM, Microsoft, Netscape, and Sun have announced plans to enter the business.
Our management team has a great deal of experience...	consuming the product or service.
A select group of investors is considering the plan.	We mailed a copy of the plan to everyone in *Pratt's Guide*.
We seek a value-added investor.	We are looking for a passive, dumb-as-rocks investor.
If you invest on our terms, you will earn a 68% internal rate of return.	If everything that could ever conceivably go right does go right, you might get your money back.

lot better about risk if the venture's endgame is discussed up front. There is an old saying, "If you don't know where you are going, any road will get you there." In crafting sensible entrepreneurial strategies, just the opposite is true: You had better know where you might end up and have a map for getting there. A business plan should be the place where that map is drawn, for, as every traveler knows, a journey is a lot less risky when you have directions.

The Deal and Beyond

Once a business plan is written, of course, the goal is to land a deal. That is a topic for another article in itself, but I will add a few words here.

When I talk to young (and old) entrepreneurs looking to finance their ventures, they obsess about the valuation and terms of the deal they will receive. Their explicit goal seems to be to minimize the dilution they will suffer in raising capital. Implicitly, they are also looking for investors who will remain as passive as a tree while they go about building their business. On the food chain of investors, it seems, doctors and dentists are best and venture capitalists are worst because of the degree to which the latter group demands control and a large share of the returns.

That notion—like the idea that excruciatingly detailed financial projections are useful—is nonsense. From whom you raise capital is often more important than the terms. New ventures are inherently risky, as I've noted; what can go wrong will. When that happens, unsophisticated investors panic, get angry, and often refuse to advance the company more money. Sophisticated investors, by contrast, roll up their sleeves and help the company solve its problems. Often, they've had lots of experience saving sinking ships. They are typically process literate. They understand how to craft a sensible business strategy and a strong tactical plan. They know how to recruit, compensate, and motivate team members. They are also familiar with the Byzantine ins and outs of going public—an event most entrepreneurs face but once in a lifetime. This kind of knowhow is worth the money needed to buy it.

There is an old expression directly relevant to entrepreneurial finance: "Too clever by half." Often, deal makers get very creative, crafting all sorts of payoff and option schemes. That usually backfires. My experience has proven again and again that sensible deals have the following six characteristics:

- They are simple.

- They are fair.

- They emphasize trust rather than legal ties.

- They do not blow apart if actual differs slightly from plan.

- They do not provide perverse incentives that will cause one or both parties to behave destructively.

- They are written on a pile of papers no greater than one-quarter inch thick.

But even these six simple rules miss an important point. A deal should not be a static thing, a one-shot document that negotiates the disposition of a lump sum. Instead, it is incumbent upon entrepreneurs, before they go searching for funding, to think about capital acquisition as a dynamic process—to figure out how much money they will need and when they will need it.

How is that accomplished? The trick is for the entrepreneurial team to treat the new venture as a series of experiments. Before launching the whole show, launch a little piece of it. Convene a focus group to test the product, build a prototype and watch it perform, conduct a regional or local rollout of a service. Such an exercise reveals the true economics of the business and can help enormously in determining how much money the new venture actually requires and in what stages. Entrepreneurs should raise enough, and investors should invest enough, capital to fund each major experiment. Experiments, of course, can feel expensive and risky. But I've seen them prevent disasters and help create successes. I consider it a prerequisite of putting together a winning deal.

Beware the Albatross

Among the many sins committed by business plan writers is arrogance. In today's economy, few ideas are truly proprietary. Moreover, there has never been a time in recorded history when the supply of capital did not outrace the supply of opportunity. The true half-life of opportunity is decreasing with the passage of time.

A business plan must not be an albatross that hangs around the neck of the entrepreneurial team, dragging it into oblivion. Instead, a business plan must be a call for action, one that recognizes management's responsibility to fix what is broken proactively and in real time. Risk is inevitable, avoiding risk impossible. Risk management is the key, always tilting the venture in favor of reward and away from risk.

A plan must demonstrate mastery of the entire entrepreneurial process, from identification of opportunity to harvest. It is not a way to separate unsuspecting investors from their money by hiding the fatal flaw. For in the final analysis, the only one being fooled is the entrepreneur.

We live today in the golden age of entrepreneurship. Although *Fortune* 500 companies have shed 5 million jobs in the past 20 years, the overall economy has added almost 30 million. Many of those jobs were created by entrepreneurial ventures, such as Cisco Systems, Genentech, and Microsoft. Each of those companies started with a business plan. Is that why they succeeded? There is no knowing for sure. But there is little doubt that crafting a business plan so that it thoroughly and candidly addresses the ingredients of success—people, opportunity, context, and the risk/reward picture—is vitally important. In the absence of a crystal ball, in fact, a business plan built of the *right* information and analysis can only be called indispensable.

Originally published in July–August 1997. Reprint 97409

Why the Lean Start-Up Changes Everything

by Steve Blank

LAUNCHING A NEW ENTERPRISE—whether it's a tech start-up, a small business, or an initiative within a large corporation—has always been a hit-or-miss proposition. According to the decades-old formula, you write a business plan, pitch it to investors, assemble a team, introduce a product, and start selling as hard as you can. And somewhere in this sequence of events, you'll probably suffer a fatal setback. The odds are not with you: As new research by Harvard Business School's Shikhar Ghosh shows, 75% of all start-ups fail.

But recently an important countervailing force has emerged, one that can make the process of starting a company less risky. It's a methodology called the "lean start-up," and it favors experimentation over elaborate planning, customer feedback over intuition, and iterative design over traditional "big design up front" development. Although the methodology is just a few years old, its concepts—such as "minimum viable product" and "pivoting"—have quickly taken root in the start-up world, and business schools have already begun adapting their curricula to teach them.

The lean start-up movement hasn't gone totally mainstream, however, and we have yet to feel its full impact. In many ways it is roughly where the big data movement was five years ago—consisting mainly of a buzzword that's not yet widely understood, whose implications companies are just beginning to grasp. But as its practices spread, they're turning the conventional wisdom about entrepreneurship on its head. New ventures of all kinds are attempting to improve their chances of success by following its principles of failing fast and continually learning. And despite the methodology's name, in the long term some of its biggest payoffs may be gained by the *large* companies that embrace it.

In this article I'll offer a brief overview of lean start-up techniques and how they've evolved. Most important, I'll explain how, in combination with other business trends, they could ignite a new entrepreneurial economy.

The Fallacy of the Perfect Business Plan

According to conventional wisdom, the first thing every founder must do is create a business plan—a static document that describes the size of an opportunity, the problem to be solved, and the solution that the new venture will provide. Typically it includes a five-year forecast for income, profits, and cash flow. A business plan is essentially a research exercise written in isolation at a desk before an entrepreneur has even begun to build a product. The assumption is that it's possible to figure out most of the unknowns of a business in advance, before you raise money and actually execute the idea.

Once an entrepreneur with a convincing business plan obtains money from investors, he or she begins developing the product in a similarly insular fashion. Developers invest thousands of man-hours to get it ready for launch, with little if any customer input. Only after building and launching the product does the venture get substantial feedback from customers—when the sales force attempts to sell it. And too often, after months or even years of development, entrepreneurs learn the hard way that customers do not need or want most of the product's features.

After decades of watching thousands of start-ups follow this standard regimen, we've now learned at least three things:

1. Business plans rarely survive first contact with customers. As the boxer Mike Tyson once said about his opponents' prefight strategies: "Everybody has a plan until they get punched in the mouth."

Idea in Brief

Over the past few years, a new methodology for launching companies, called the "lean start-up," has begun to replace the old regimen.

Instead of executing business plans, operating in stealth mode, and releasing fully functional prototypes, young ventures are testing hypotheses, gathering early and frequent customer feedback, and showing "minimum viable products" to prospects. This new process recognizes that searching for a business model (which is the primary task facing a start-up) is entirely different from executing against that model (which is what established firms do).

Recently, business schools have begun to teach the methodology, which can also be learned at events such as Startup Weekend. Over time, lean start-up techniques could reduce the failure rate of new ventures and, in combination with other trends taking hold in the business world, launch a new, more entrepreneurial economy.

2. No one besides venture capitalists and the late Soviet Union requires five-year plans to forecast complete unknowns. These plans are generally fiction, and dreaming them up is almost always a waste of time.

3. Start-ups are not smaller versions of large companies. They do not unfold in accordance with master plans. The ones that ultimately succeed go quickly from failure to failure, all the while adapting, iterating on, and improving their initial ideas as they continually learn from customers.

One of the critical differences is that while existing companies *execute* a business model, start-ups *look* for one. This distinction is at the heart of the lean start-up approach. It shapes the lean definition of a start-up: a temporary organization designed to search for a repeatable and scalable business model.

The lean method has three key principles:

First, rather than engaging in months of planning and research, entrepreneurs accept that all they have on day one is a series of untested hypotheses—basically, good guesses. So instead of writing an intricate business plan, founders summarize their hypotheses in

Sketch out your hypotheses

The business model canvas lets you look at all nine building blocks of your business on one page. Each component of the business model contains a series of hypotheses that you need to test.

Key partners	Key activities	Value propositions	Customer relationships	Customer segments
Who are our key partners? Who are our key suppliers? Which key resources are we acquiring from our partners? Which key activities do partners perform?	What key activities do our value propositions require? Our distribution channels? Customer relationships? Revenue streams?	What value do we deliver to the customer? Which one of our customers' problems are we helping to solve? What bundles of products and services are we offering to each segment? Which customer needs are we satisfying? What is the minimum viable product?	How do we get, keep, and grow customers? Which customer relationships have we established? How are they integrated with the rest of our business model? How costly are they?	For whom are we creating value? Who are our most important customers? What are the customer archetypes?
	Key resources		**Channels**	
	What key resources do our value propositions require? Our distribution channels? Customer relationships? Revenue streams?		Through which channels do our customer segments want to be reached? How do other companies reach them now? Which ones work best? Which ones are most cost-efficient? How are we integrating them with customer routines?	

Cost structure		Revenue streams	
What are the most important costs inherent to our business model? Which key resources are most expensive? Which key activities are most expensive?		For what value are our customers really willing to pay? For what do they currently pay? What is the revenue model? What are the pricing tactics?	

Source: www.businessmodelgeneration.com/canvas. Canvas concept developed by Alexander Osterwalder and Yves Pigneur.

a framework called a *business model canvas*. Essentially, this is a diagram of how a company creates value for itself and its customers. (See the exhibit "Sketch out your hypotheses.")

Second, lean start-ups use a "get out of the building" approach called *customer development* to test their hypotheses. They go out and ask potential users, purchasers, and partners for feedback on all elements of the business model, including product features, pricing, distribution channels, and affordable customer acquisition strategies. The emphasis is on nimbleness and speed: New ventures rapidly assemble minimum viable products and immediately elicit customer feedback. Then, using customers' input to revise their assumptions, they start the cycle over again, testing redesigned offerings and making further small adjustments (iterations) or more substantive ones (pivots) to ideas that aren't working. (See the exhibit "Listen to customers.")

Third, lean start-ups practice something called *agile development,* which originated in the software industry. Agile development works hand-in-hand with customer development. Unlike typical yearlong product development cycles that presuppose knowledge of customers' problems and product needs, agile development eliminates wasted time and resources by developing the product iteratively and incrementally. It's the process by which start-ups create the minimum viable products they test. (See the exhibit "Quick, responsive development.")

When Jorge Heraud and Lee Redden started Blue River Technology, they were students in my class at Stanford. They had a vision of building robotic lawn mowers for commercial spaces. After talking to over 100 customers in 10 weeks, they learned their initial customer target—golf courses—didn't value their solution. But then they began to talk to farmers and found a huge demand for an automated way to kill weeds without chemicals. Filling it became their new product focus, and within 10 weeks Blue River had built and tested a prototype. Nine months later the start-up had obtained more than $3 million in venture funding. The team expected to have a commercial product ready just nine months after that.

Listen to customers

During customer development, a start-up searches for a business model that works. If customer feedback reveals that its business hypotheses are wrong, it either revises them or "pivots" to new hypotheses. Once a model is proven, the start-up starts executing, building a formal organization. Each stage of customer development is iterative: A start-up will probably fail several times before finding the right approach.

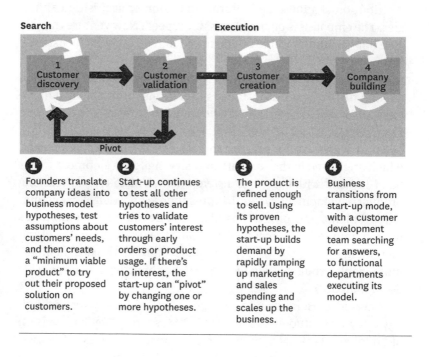

Search

Execution

| 1 Customer discovery | 2 Customer validation | 3 Customer creation | 4 Company building |

Pivot

1 Founders translate company ideas into business model hypotheses, test assumptions about customers' needs, and then create a "minimum viable product" to try out their proposed solution on customers.

2 Start-up continues to test all other hypotheses and tries to validate customers' interest through early orders or product usage. If there's no interest, the start-up can "pivot" by changing one or more hypotheses.

3 The product is refined enough to sell. Using its proven hypotheses, the start-up builds demand by rapidly ramping up marketing and sales spending and scales up the business.

4 Business transitions from start-up mode, with a customer development team searching for answers, to functional departments executing its model.

Stealth Mode's Declining Popularity

Lean methods are changing the language start-ups use to describe their work. During the dot-com boom, start-ups often operated in "stealth mode" (to avoid alerting potential competitors to a market opportunity), exposing prototypes to customers only during highly orchestrated "beta" tests. The lean start-up methodology makes those concepts obsolete because it holds that in most industries

Quick, responsive development

In contrast to traditional product development, in which each stage occurs in linear order and lasts for months, agile development builds products in short, repeated cycles. A start-up produces a "minimum viable product"—containing only critical features—gathers feedback on it from customers, and then starts over with a revised minimum viable product.

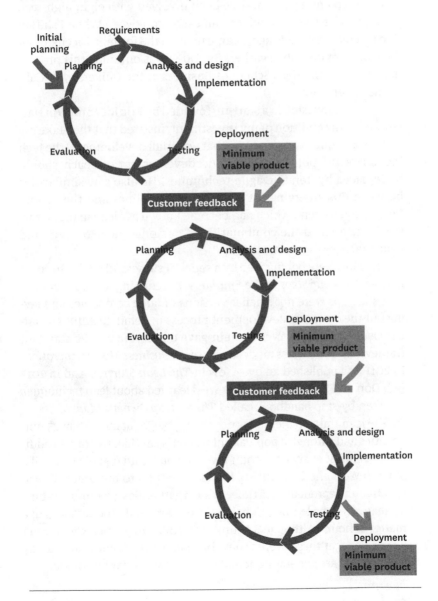

customer feedback matters more than secrecy and that constant feedback yields better results than cadenced unveilings.

Those two fundamental precepts crystallized for me during my career as an entrepreneur. (I've been involved with eight high-tech start-ups, as either a founder or an early employee.) When I shifted into teaching, a decade ago, I came up with the formula for customer development described earlier. By 2003 I was outlining this process in a course at the Haas School of Business at the University of California at Berkeley.

In 2004, I invested in a start-up founded by Eric Ries and Will Harvey and, as a condition of my investment, insisted that they take my course. Eric quickly recognized that waterfall development, the tech industry's traditional, linear product development approach, should be replaced by iterative agile techniques. He also saw similarities between this emerging set of start-up disciplines and the Toyota Production System, which had become known as "lean manufacturing." Eric dubbed the combination of customer development and agile practices the "lean start-up."

The tools were popularized by a series of successful books. In 2003, I wrote *The Four Steps to the Epiphany,* articulating for the first time that start-ups were not smaller versions of large companies and laying out the customer development process in detail. In 2010, Alexander Osterwalder and Yves Pigneur gave entrepreneurs the standard framework for business model canvases in *Business Model Generation.* In 2011 Eric published an overview in *The Lean Startup.* And in 2012 Bob Dorf and I summarized what we'd learned about lean techniques in a step-by-step handbook called *The Startup Owner's Manual.*

The lean start-up method is now being taught at more than 25 universities and through a popular online course at Udacity.com. In addition, in almost every city around world, you'll find organizations like Startup Weekend introducing the lean method to hundreds of prospective entrepreneurs at a time. At such gatherings a roomful of start-up teams can cycle through half a dozen potential product ideas in a matter of hours. Although it sounds incredible to people who haven't been to one, at these events some businesses are formed on a Friday evening and are generating actual revenue by Sunday afternoon.

Creating an Entrepreneurial, Innovation-Based Economy

While some adherents claim that the lean process can make individual start-ups more successful, I believe that claim is too grandiose. Success is predicated on too many factors for one methodology to guarantee that any single start-up will be a winner. But on the basis of what I've seen at hundreds of start-ups, at programs that teach lean principles, and at established companies that practice them, I can make a more important claim: Using lean methods across a portfolio of start-ups will result in fewer failures than using traditional methods.

A lower start-up failure rate could have profound economic consequences. Today the forces of disruption, globalization, and regulation are buffeting the economies of every country. Established industries are rapidly shedding jobs, many of which will never return. Employment growth in the 21st century will have to come from new ventures, so we all have a vested interest in fostering an environment that helps them succeed, grow, and hire more workers. The creation of an innovation economy that's driven by the rapid expansion of start-ups has never been more imperative.

In the past, growth in the number of start-ups was constrained by five factors in addition to the failure rate:

1. The high cost of getting the first customer and the even higher cost of getting the product wrong.

2. Long technology development cycles.

3. The limited number of people with an appetite for the risks inherent in founding or working at a start-up.

4. The structure of the venture capital industry, in which a small number of firms each needed to invest big sums in a handful of start-ups to have a chance at significant returns.

5. The concentration of real expertise in how to build start-ups, which in the United States was mostly found in pockets on the East and West coasts. (This is less an issue in Europe and other parts of the world, but even overseas there are geographic entrepreneurial hot spots.)

What Lean Start-Ups Do Differently

THE FOUNDERS OF LEAN START-UPS don't begin with a business plan; they begin with the search for a business model. Only after quick rounds of experimentation and feedback reveal a model that works do lean founders focus on execution.

Lean	Traditional
STRATEGY	
Business model Hypothesis-driven	**Business plan** Implementation-driven
NEW-PRODUCT PROCESS	
Customer development Get out of the office and test hypotheses	**Product management** Prepare offering for market following a linear, step-by-step plan
ENGINEERING	
Agile development Build the product iteratively and incrementally	**Agile or waterfall development** Build the product iteratively, or fully specify the product before building it
ORGANIZATION	
Customer and agile development teams Hire for learning, nimbleness, and speed	**Departments by function** Hire for experience and ability to execute
FINANCIAL REPORTING	
Metrics that matter Customer acquisition cost, lifetime customer value, churn, viralness	**Accounting** Income statement, balance sheet, cash flow statement
FAILURE	
Expected Fix by iterating on ideas and pivoting away from ones that don't work	**Exception** Fix by firing executives
SPEED	
Rapid Operates on good-enough data	**Measured** Operates on complete data

The lean approach reduces the first two constraints by helping new ventures launch products that customers actually want, far more quickly and cheaply than traditional methods, and the third by making start-ups less risky. And it has emerged at a time when other business and technology trends are likewise breaking down the barriers to start-up formation. The combination of all these forces is altering the entrepreneurial landscape.

Today open source software, like GitHub, and cloud services, such as Amazon Web Services, have slashed the cost of software development from millions of dollars to thousands. Hardware start-ups no longer have to build their own factories, since offshore manufacturers are so easily accessible. Indeed, it's become quite common to see young tech companies that practice the lean start-up methodology offer software products that are simply "bits" delivered over the web or hardware that's built in China within weeks of being formed. Consider Roominate, a start-up designed to inspire girls' confidence and interest in science, technology, engineering, and math. Once its founders had finished testing and iterating on the design of their wired dollhouse kit, they sent the specs off to a contract manufacturer in China. Three weeks later the first products arrived.

Another important trend is the decentralization of access to financing. Venture capital used to be a tight club of formal firms clustered near Silicon Valley, Boston, and New York. In today's entrepreneurial ecosystem, new super angel funds, smaller than the traditional hundred-million-dollar-sized VC fund, can make early-stage investments. Worldwide, hundreds of accelerators, like Y Combinator and TechStars, have begun to formalize seed investments. And crowdsourcing sites like Kickstarter provide another, more democratic method of financing start-ups.

The instantaneous availability of information is also a boon to today's new ventures. Before the internet, new company founders got advice only as often as they could have coffee with experienced investors or entrepreneurs. Today the biggest challenge is sorting through the overwhelming amount of start-up advice they get. The lean concepts provide a framework that helps you differentiate the good from the bad.

Lean start-up techniques were initially designed to create fast-growing tech ventures. But I believe the concepts are equally valid for creating the Main Street small businesses that make up the bulk of the economy. If the entire universe of small business embraced them, I strongly suspect it would increase growth and efficiency, and have a direct and immediate impact on GDP and employment.

There are signs that this may in fact happen. In 2011 the U.S. National Science Foundation began using lean methods to commercialize basic science research in a program called the Innovation Corps. Eleven universities now teach the methods to hundreds of teams of senior research scientists across the United States.

MBA programs are adopting these techniques, too. For years they taught students to apply large-company approaches—such as accounting methods for tracking revenue and cash flow, and organizational theories about managing—to start-ups. Yet start-ups face completely different issues. Now business schools are realizing that new ventures need their own management tools.

As business schools embrace the distinction between management execution and searching for a business model, they're abandoning the business plan as the template for entrepreneurial education. And the business plan competitions that have been a celebrated part of the MBA experience for over a decade are being replaced by business model competitions. (Harvard Business School became the latest to make this switch, in 2012.) Stanford, Harvard, Berkeley, and Columbia are leading the charge and embracing the lean start-up curriculum. My Lean LaunchPad course for educators is now training over 250 college and university instructors a year.

A New Strategy for the 21st-Century Corporation

It's already becoming clear that lean start-up practices are not just for young tech ventures.

Corporations have spent the past 20 years increasing their efficiency by driving down costs. But simply focusing on improving existing business models is not enough anymore. Almost every large company understands that it also needs to deal with ever-increasing external threats by continually innovating. To ensure their survival and growth, corporations need to keep inventing new business models. This challenge requires entirely new organizational structures and skills.

Over the years managerial experts such as Clayton Christensen, Rita McGrath, Vijay Govindarajan, Henry Chesbrough, Ian MacMillan, Alexander Osterwalder, and Eric von Hippel have advanced the thinking on how large companies can improve their innovation processes. During the past three years, however, we have seen large companies, including General Electric, Qualcomm, and Intuit, begin to implement the lean start-up methodology.

GE's Energy Storage division, for instance, is using the approach to transform the way it innovates. In 2010 Prescott Logan, the general manager of the division, recognized that a new battery developed by the unit had the potential to disrupt the industry. Instead of preparing to build a factory, scale up production, and launch the new offering (ultimately named Durathon) as a traditional product extension, Logan applied lean techniques. He started searching for a business model and engaging in customer discovery. He and his team met face-to-face with dozens of global prospects to explore potential new markets and applications. These weren't sales calls: The team members left their PowerPoint slides behind and listened to customers' issues and frustrations with the battery status quo. They dug deep to learn how customers bought industrial batteries, how often they used them, and the operating conditions. With this feedback, they made a major shift in their customer focus. They eliminated one of their initial target segments, data centers, and discovered a new one—utilities. In addition, they narrowed the broad customer segment of "telecom" to cell phone providers in developing countries with unreliable electric grids. Eventually GE invested $100 million to build a world-class battery manufacturing facility in Schenectady, New York, which it opened in 2012. According to press reports, demand for the new batteries is so high that GE is already running a backlog of orders.

The first hundred years of management education focused on building strategies and tools that formalized execution and efficiency for existing businesses. Now, we have the first set of tools for searching for new business models as we launch start-up ventures. It also happens to have arrived just in time to help existing companies deal with the forces of continual disruption. In the 21st century those forces will make people in every kind of organization—start-ups, small businesses, corporations, and government—feel the pressure of rapid change. The lean start-up approach will help them meet it head-on, innovate rapidly, and transform business as we know it.

Originally published in May 2013. Reprint R1305C

The President of SRI Ventures on Bringing Siri to Life

by Norman Winarsky

IN THE LONG PROCESS OF DESIGNING and perfecting a product, there's often a single moment when a potential customer's reaction helps overcome the doubts that surround any creative endeavor. For Siri, the virtual personal assistant that's now an integral part of Apple's iPhone, that moment came on an airplane in 2009. I had just taken my seat on a delayed flight when a passenger asked what time we were expected to land. Since I was one of a few dozen people testing Siri, I took out my phone and said, "Siri, what time is United Flight 98 expected to arrive?" When Siri responded with the updated arrival time, the passenger looked stunned. He said, "I have only one question: Why are you sitting in coach? You ought to be a billionaire!"

I had been so deeply immersed in the venture's business, technological, strategic, and financial challenges that I had lost sight of how dazzling the Siri technology was. It took a stranger's dropped jaw to remind me: We had developed a smartphone application that could understand and answer questions using natural language. We were going to put artificial intelligence into millions of consumers' hands.

It had been a long road with a couple of surprising turns.

The Valley of Death

As president at SRI International, an organization founded in 1946 as Stanford Research Institute (and independent since 1970), I lead the group that creates, builds, and spins off ventures from SRI technology. I have an amazing job. Every day I watch the development of breakthrough technologies with the potential to make people safer, healthier, and more productive.

But a valley of death lies between invention and innovation. This is a common metaphor in the venture world, because most inventions perish before reaching the marketplace, for lack of a large and growing market, a strong value proposition and business plan, or sufficient resources.

It's my job to help opportunities cross this valley of death. Sometimes we succeed beyond our wildest dreams. Siri was indeed a stunning breakthrough.

The market vision that led to Siri goes back to 2003, when a mobile phone's primary applications were still limited to ringtones and messaging. We recognized that the phone's growing capabilities would eventually put a communicating supercomputer in everyone's pocket, and we believed that SRI International was well suited to be a leader in the inevitable technology and market revolution.

We formed a team, dubbed Vanguard, to develop market concepts. Some early ones were to put intelligence into the smartphone so that users could ask it by text or voice to perform tasks, such as scheduling a call among multiple parties, placing a call, or ordering groceries.

At about the same time the Vanguard team was formed, the U.S. Defense Advanced Research Projects Agency (DARPA) funded a $150 million program to develop a "cognitive" software assistant. (One inspiration was Radar O'Reilly, of the TV series *M*A*S*H,* who always knew what his colonel wanted before the colonel did.) Concepts from the DARPA program contributed to Vanguard's thinking and ultimately helped inspire Siri.

Over the next four years creating a stand-alone venture was not our goal: We talked to dozens of telecom carriers and handset providers, with the aim of starting a joint project that would license

Idea in Brief

The market vision that led to Siri, the virtual personal assistant that's now an integral part of Apple's iPhone, can be traced back to 2003, when a mobile phone's primary applications were still limited to ringtones and messaging. The author and his colleagues at SRI International recognized that the phone's growing capabilities would eventually put a communicating supercomputer in everyone's pocket. They believed that their company was well suited to be a leader in the inevitable technology and market revolution—as it had been in every previous computing revolution.

They didn't originally plan to create a stand-alone venture.

They talked to dozens of telecom carriers and handset providers, with the aim of jointly starting a project that would license the technology. But because the few resulting commercial projects implemented only small parts of its original vision, the founding team decided to drop that idea and create and build its own venture. Speech-to-text was the easy part: SRI had launched Nuance, a world leader in speech solutions. The hard part was analyzing words so as to understand the user's intent and then reason about and answer the request. The runaway success of Siri demonstrates how well the team met that challenge.

our technology and deploy an intelligent assistant in the commercial world. This turned out to be difficult. Again and again we heard various objections: "Not possible: The technology is 20 years away." "Too expensive" (we were seeking $5 million to $10 million in development funding, plus licensing fees). "Not part of our business model." "Creating a product will take longer than 12 months." "Not an early source of revenue." "We're already doing it ourselves." We did a few projects with companies that implemented small parts of our vision, but ultimately we decided to spin off a venture from SRI to create a whole new product category.

The Four Ingredients

The founding team of SRI business and technology leaders met almost daily in SRI's venture space to discuss the market and product possibilities. We knew that to succeed we needed four major

A hothouse of innovation

SRI has helped invent technologies vital to industries as varied as aerospace, aviation, banking, and telecommunications. A sampling:

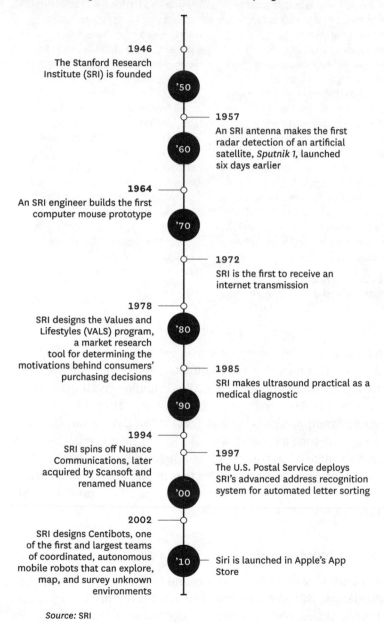

1946
The Stanford Research Institute (SRI) is founded

1957
An SRI antenna makes the first radar detection of an artificial satellite, *Sputnik 1,* launched six days earlier

1964
An SRI engineer builds the first computer mouse prototype

1972
SRI is the first to receive an internet transmission

1978
SRI designs the Values and Lifestyles (VALS) program, a market research tool for determining the motivations behind consumers' purchasing decisions

1985
SRI makes ultrasound practical as a medical diagnostic

1994
SRI spins off Nuance Communications, later acquired by Scansoft and renamed Nuance

1997
The U.S. Postal Service deploys SRI's advanced address recognition system for automated letter sorting

2002
SRI designs Centibots, one of the first and largest teams of coordinated, autonomous mobile robots that can explore, map, and survey unknown environments

Siri is launched in Apple's App Store

Source: SRI

ingredients: a solution to a large and important problem or pain point, with potential for rapid market growth; a differentiated technology that would trump the competition; a team capable of outstanding execution; and a value proposition and business plan that would articulate the venture's strategy and value. Without all four, the probability of success would be nearly zero.

We also knew that we had only a short time and limited financial resources to enter and succeed in the market before we ran out of money or competitors emerged.

The pain point

Over several months the team zeroed in on the market opportunity: People were frustrated by all the keyboard clicking needed for any task on a smartphone. (Clicking on smartphones was not yet natural in 2007.) Market research found that each time users had to click through a screen, 20% abandoned the application or purchase intent.

The breakthrough idea behind Siri was simple and powerful: In contrast to search engines, Siri would be a voice-driven "do engine." It would understand your query, automatically access the information needed, and distill it into an answer. All the effort would be made by Siri rather than by the user—it would be a virtual personal assistant that would help people buy tickets to a ball game, make a dinner reservation, get a weather report, or find a movie with one or two clicks.

The differentiated technology

The technology needed to address the pain point was daunting, even though decades of development were behind it. Converting speech to digital text was the easy part: SRI had launched Nuance, a world leader in speech solutions, in 1994. The hard part was analyzing words so as to understand the user's intent and then reason about and respond to the request. The computer had to identify concepts and associate groups of words with them. Humans perform such tasks easily, but most people believed they were impossible for computers.

The broad basis for technology to understand natural language had been developed by the SRI Speech Technology and Research Lab and SRI's Artificial Intelligence Center in programs with DARPA, and by SRI's internal investments. Adam Cheyer and Didier Guzzoni led the specific implementation that allowed us to make Siri a product that could be deployed to millions. For almost two decades Cheyer, one of SRI's most visionary computer scientists, had designed and implemented delegated computing and "agent-based systems" that let humans interact with networked programs and devices. With Guzzoni, his PhD student, he developed approaches for natural-language understanding and reasoning that simplified the task of responding to queries.

The team

We were fortunate to recruit an outstanding entrepreneur, Dag Kittlaus, to be the new venture's CEO. Cheyer chose to leave SRI and join the venture. Tom Gruber, a leading innovator in intelligent user interfaces, joined a few months later and eventually became the CTO. Bill Mark, the president of information and computing sciences at SRI, and I were the other founders. We two remained at SRI, and I became a board member of the new venture.

The value proposition

Over the six months the overall value proposition came into sharp focus: We would solve a major problem for millions of consumers with a powerful product that could generate billions of dollars in revenue. Specifically, Siri would relieve the pain of too many clicks; save people time and energy; provide a differentiated and break-through technology through speech recognition, natural-language understanding, and artificial intelligence; provide revenue-generating uses; and surprise and delight consumers. We decided that Siri's business model would be dependent on collecting fees from websites for helping to execute transactions. We recognized that revenue from the leads Siri provided to hotels, restaurants, and airlines could be substantial.

In late 2007, after six months of crafting the value proposition, we decided to seek outside investment for our spin-off venture. We knew that finding backers would not be easy, because Siri depended on breakthroughs in both market and technology. Many venture capitalists had seen the hype versus reality for AI and were skeptical. They worried about every element of the value proposition and business plan, including market, technology, and competitors. Would we be able to grow a large consumer base? Would the processing power of the smartphone be sufficient? Would the AI technology work? Would communication and processing be too slow? Would the lead generation business model produce enough revenue? Would potential competitors, such as Google and Microsoft, respond rapidly with their own products?

In the end, concerns can only be mitigated, not eliminated. Siri would be a bold but risky investment. It would clearly have an impact on the mobile industry with its disruptive technology—the result of a remarkable convergence of worldwide trends, including the emergence of smartphones; the acceleration of computing and storage capacity and communication speed; the growth of web services and interfaces; and the development of new AI systems. The time was right.

We raised $8.5 million—enough to fund the venture for 18 months. The funding process gave us far more than money, however. It gave us courageous, insightful investors who became our partners, helping us identify business models, develop strategy, build relationships with customers, and more.

Still, we faced many challenges: We were delayed for six months by issues relating to the slow server-to-user response and the speech recognition technology. In the meantime, Google and others were making progress on their own solutions. Some companies made offers to acquire us. Deal terms with providers and web services companies were complex. Wireless carriers emerged with opportunities that distracted from our initial product.

The Launch

Finally, after user testing from November 2009 to February 2010 (during which I showed off Siri on that airplane), we were ready to launch in Apple's App Store. (That "Siri" is close in spelling to "SRI" is pure coincidence. We chose the name for several reasons, including that it was just four letters and did not have negative connotations in any language.) We had prepared with demonstrations and reviews by top bloggers from sites such as Scobleizer and TechCrunch. The demonstrations were a great success, and the press created an avalanche of consumer interest. Siri was downloaded free at an astronomical rate. It was in the top 50 of all Apple apps and was the top lifestyle app.

Two weeks after the launch, Kittlaus received an unexpected phone call: "Hi, this is Steve Jobs." Kittlaus thought it was a joke and hung up. Then the phone rang again: "Really, it's Steve Jobs." It was. The two talked for a while, and Jobs congratulated Kittlaus on Siri's capability. He invited Kittlaus, Cheyer, and Gruber to his house, where they discussed Siri's technology. Jobs understood the value of the engine's AI as well as the nature of the technology and the certainty that errors, such as in recognition of natural language, would always occur—but he was not discouraged. That seemed

SRI International facts and financials

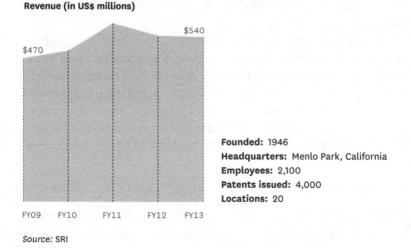

Revenue (in US$ millions)

$540

$470

FY09 FY10 FY11 FY12 FY13

Founded: 1946
Headquarters: Menlo Park, California
Employees: 2,100
Patents issued: 4,000
Locations: 20

Source: SRI

remarkable, because virtually all Apple products are designed "for perfection."

Over the next few weeks Jobs and Kittlaus discussed a purchase price for Siri. We were not eager to sell, because we believed the value of the business would almost certainly increase with successful trials and new distribution deals. But Jobs made an offer that the investors and the executive team couldn't refuse. (The price cannot be revealed because of contractual obligations.) The team was also deeply attracted to working with Jobs and Apple.

A year later Siri became the core platform for a highly popular service on Apple's new iPhone 4S. On October 4, 2011, Phil Schiller, Apple's SVP of worldwide marketing, introduced Siri as the "coolest feature of the iPhone 4S." The next day, Steve Jobs died. I'm grateful that he got to see the presentation. In the first few weeks postlaunch, analysts reported that Siri helped to accelerate billions of dollars' worth of sales. Siri remains a core element of all Apple's iOS devices.

Apple and many other companies, including SRI, are now in a race to develop products that both advance the technology and serve new markets. Much can be done. Speech and natural-language recognition and machine learning are still in their infancy. New virtual personal assistants will be even better at word and language understanding. They will maintain context, enable true conversations, learn from their users, and become "specialists" helping consumers access information such as health records and bank accounts. For example, SRI recently launched a new venture, Kasisto, that is redefining the mobile banking experience through speech, text, and touch interfaces and has the capacity for conversation. The future of virtual personal assistants is unquestionably secure.

Originally published in September 2015. Reprint R1509A

In Search of the Next Big Thing

An interview with Marc Andreessen.
by Adi Ignatius

MARC ANDREESSEN KNOWS both sides of the start-up game. As freshly minted university graduates in the 1990s, he and his partners went hat in hand to venture capitalists in Silicon Valley to fund their new project, the breakthrough web browser Netscape Navigator. Within 18 months the enterprise had gone public and Andreessen had become a symbol of the internet generation. Now he's a cofounder and partner of Andreessen Horowitz, a Menlo Park venture capital fund that's trying to make smart bets on tech start-ups in a climate much icier than the one during the dot-com boom. In this edited interview with HBR's editor in chief, Adi Ignatius, Andreessen talks about the complex challenges entrepreneurs now face and an investment opportunity that slipped away.

HBR: *How would you characterize the best entrepreneurs you work with?*

Andreessen: We aim for a trifecta in the people we want to back. We're trying to find a product innovator who is entrepreneurial and wants to start a company, and who also has the bandwidth and discipline to become a CEO. When people like that actually deliver and work hard for 10 years, the results are miraculous. If they fall down on any of those three fronts, generally it's a casualty.

Do all those skills really have to reside in one person?

It's hard to pair a product innovator with a business partner—or to partner the founder with an outside CEO—and have them get anywhere. We work with our companies when they absolutely have to do this, but it's very challenging.

Can entrepreneurs be taught? Or are the skills innate?

We think CEOs can be taught, so we specialize in training innovators to become CEOs. We don't spend a lot of time trying to teach CEOs to be innovators.

To what extent is the start-up business still hung-over from the last boom and bust in tech stocks?

It's a really big deal, especially for anybody over age 35. It's similar to what happened after the Great Depression: Not until the 1950s did people really start focusing again on the stock market. Everybody's hypersensitive about another bubble. The minute anything starts to show even a little bit of life, they say, "Oh, my God, it's another bubble!"

Are you saying that the general view of the market is irrational?

Yeah, it's irrational. The rational thing is to focus on the future, not the past. But current attitudes are very much based on what happened in the past.

What's the view of Andreessen Horowitz?

Obviously, we see opportunity. We started our firm in 2009, after probably the worst 10 years ever in venture capital. But given the history of these things, this is probably a good time to get in.

Do you see the danger of a new bubble out there?

It's in the nature of venture capital and start-up investing that there are always stupid investments. The problem is that you never know which ones are which. I get these things as wrong as anybody else. But if you're afraid to make any investments that might be stupid,

Idea in Brief

In the 1990s, just out of college, Andreessen went knocking on VC doors in Silicon Valley, looking to fund what became the breakthrough web browser Netscape Navigator. Within 18 months the company had gone public and he'd become a symbol of the internet generation. Now he's a cofounder and partner of Andreessen Horowitz, a venture capital fund that looks for smart tech start-ups. In this edited interview he talks with HBR's editor in chief about what kind of entrepreneur his firm likes to fund, why start-ups are still feeling the effects of the last boom and bust in tech stocks, what they should do to prepare for an IPO, the role of hedge funds, and more.

you'll never get any big winners—because the big outlier winners tend to look crazy at the start.

One symptom of the hangover is that fewer start-ups are doing IPOs. What does that mean for investors like you?

In a sense it's good for me. As venture capitalists, we have a 13-year lockup on our money, so we take "long term" seriously. I tell our entrepreneurs, "If you build a big successful independent company, at some point you almost certainly will go public."

In the meantime, how do you prepare them for that moment?

I tell them they shouldn't even think about going public until they've built what I call a fortress. You build a company that's so big and powerful and well defended that it can withstand the pressures of being public. Our entrepreneurs are therefore almost completely focused on the substance of what they're doing—as opposed to what happened in 1999, when everyone tried to take companies public in two years on the basis of a lot of hype.

Ah, the good old days.

One of the local VCs had two mottoes in 1999. One was "Grow big or go home." The other was "Forget details, just do deals." The second one got them into trouble because some of their companies had very little substance. They were largely just press releases on their way to an IPO.

So walk us through getting to an IPO today.

We take companies through what we call the parade of horrors—all the stuff that happens to a public company. We take them through Sarbanes-Oxley, financial disclosure, patent laws, antitrust. We talk about what hedge funds do, and the intersection between hedge funds and fair disclosure.

What role do hedge funds play in all of this?

Hedge funds are much more powerful than they used to be. Market manipulation is never prosecuted, so they can lie about you all they want. On the short side, they target companies that aren't fully funded. If you have liquidity exposure on your balance sheet and you have to raise money at some point in the future, they'll try to kill you. And they can make it into a self-fulfilling prophecy, where it's impossible for you to raise money. So we talk a lot about what it means to have a strong balance sheet, to ensure you never get into that situation.

How much cash should a start-up have on hand?

Generally, you want to have at least two years' worth of cash on the balance sheet in case your revenue goes to zero. This is the tech industry—sometimes that actually happens.

In this brutal environment, how important is it for start-ups to retain their founders?

We always want control to rest with the founders. Anything else can be intensely dangerous, because of the ease with which people can mount proxy fights and all this other stuff. Large tech companies will often move to take over start-ups with no intention of actually buying them, just to screw up their business for 18 months.

Man, I'm glad I'm on the East Coast.

It's like World War III out here. [Laughs.]

Marc Andreessen's career

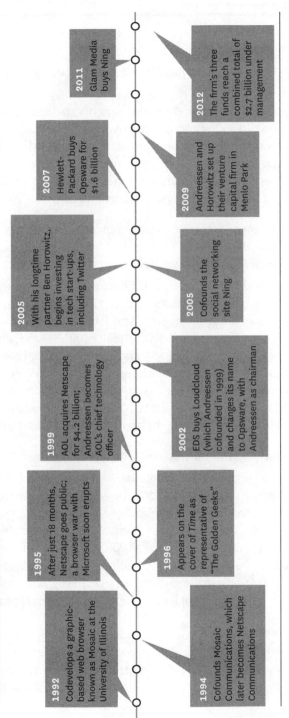

1992 — Codevelops a graphic-based web browser known as Mosaic at the University of Illinois

1994 — Cofounds Mosaic Communications, which later becomes Netscape Communications

1995 — After just 18 months, Netscape goes public; a browser war with Microsoft soon erupts

1996 — Appears on the cover of *Time* as representative of "The Golden Geeks"

1999 — AOL acquires Netscape for $4.2 billion; Andreessen becomes AOL's chief technology officer

2002 — EDS buys Loudcloud (which Andreessen cofounded in 1999) and changes its name to Opsware, with Andreessen as chairman

2005 — With his longtime partner Ben Horowitz, begins investing in tech start-ups, including Twitter

2005 — Cofounds the social networking site Ning

2007 — Hewlett-Packard buys Opsware for $1.6 billion

2009 — Andreessen and Horowitz set up their venture capital firm in Menlo Park

2011 — Glam Media buys Ning

2012 — The firm's three funds reach a combined total of $2.7 billion under management

If IPOs are so hard to pull off, are most of today's start-ups looking to sell out to bigger fish?

If somebody comes in here and says his goal is to sell his company, we won't invest. There are plenty of other venture capitalists who will fund him. For us, companies that are built to be independent are the most attractive. As for companies that are built to be sold, most acquirers are pretty smart and can smell that. It's ironic, but it's very hard for such a company to actually find a buyer.

Back in 1995, you took Netscape public after just 18 months. Now you're on the board of Facebook, which had its own noteworthy IPO. Can you talk about the difference in IPO expectations?

Netscape was a different era. There was no Sarbanes-Oxley, no reg FD [regulation fair disclosure]. Hedge funds were a tiny percentage of the market. Short sellers were small and unsophisticated. And there were more long investors who really understood what it was like to invest in a small company and see it develop. There was also the expectation that you took things public quickly. I can't really talk in detail about Facebook. But in my opinion, Facebook went public when it had become a fortress. The company had built itself into a position of strength in all the areas that make it safe to be public.

How has the lean start-up model changed the game?

It's a direct reaction to "Forget details, just do deals." Back in 1999, entrepreneurs were guided to do a fast start-up: Get the most basic, rudimentary product on the market as soon as you possibly can, and then hype the s--- out of it. Sell the s--- out of it. Try to generate as much noise as you can and as much hype as you can and get the big IPO first-day pop. And then hope that in the fullness of time you'll grow into all the promises you've made to everybody. Or, the cynics would say, you can sell out quickly. A lot of these companies had terrible products.

And now?

The new start-up methodology is basically a complete 180 on that. It says the only thing that matters is getting the product right—developing a product that people want and use and love and will pay for—before you do all the other stuff. That is a tremendously healthy move, because it centers these companies on the substance of what they're building.

Is there any downside to that kind of focus?

It can be taken too far. A large number of founders are terrified of actually getting into a market. They use this approach as an excuse to never think about sales and marketing. In my view, they're in complete denial about what it takes to actually build a company and build a business.

So what do you do? A guy comes in with a great product and no interest in the rest of it . . .

We administer a beating. [Laughs.] We basically say, Look, we understand. A 28-year-old who has built a great product and comes in here is not going to have much experience in sales and marketing. We explain that a lot of products are being sold and marketed out there. If you don't take sales and marketing seriously, nobody is ever going to know about you. Nobody is ever going to buy the thing. You're going to end up losing. But if you want to take it seriously, here are the things we can do to help you.

What are you looking for when you invest in a tech start-up?

I define a tech start-up as a new company whose value is the innovation it's bringing to the world. It's not the value of the product it's currently building but the value of the products it's going to build in the future. So it's worth investing in a technology company only if it's going to be an innovation factory for years to come.

You've written that "software is eating the world," that digital innovation is transforming virtually every industry. Where are we in that process?

It's a long-term thing. Only recently have we become a world in which everybody has a computer and we're really there with the smartphone. Now is the time when a number of industries that historically have not been much affected by technology are all of a sudden in a position to be transformed by it.

What are some examples?

The book industry is an obvious one. First Amazon came for the book distribution business. It turned that into software—the Amazon website. Now it's turning the book itself into software. We look at industries like real estate, agriculture, education, financial services, health care, retail. And we think now is a good time to create the kind of state-of-the-art software companies that will really transform them. Ironically, a lot of these companies are actually replays of ideas that were tried and failed in the dot-com era.

You've talked about having launched some big ideas that didn't fly because they were ahead of their time.

We launched Loudcloud in 1999, and basically Amazon Web Services is what Loudcloud would have been if it had launched in 2006 instead of 1999. The technology wasn't ready. Reid Hoffman started a social networking company in 1997 called SocialNet.com, long before Facebook or LinkedIn [which Hoffman cofounded in 2003] existed. For 20 years people laughed at the Apple Newton and said it proved that nobody had any interest in a tablet. And then along came the iPad. A lot of ideas that failed in the dot-com era were actually winners. They were just too early.

Does access to the cloud and big data improve the odds of success for new companies, by allowing their business models to rely a bit more on science and a bit less on art?

Yeah, I think so. The best of the companies we're seeing now are unbelievably good at analytics. They have this incredible closed loop where they analyze data and feed the numbers directly back into the process virtually in real time, running a continuous improvement loop. But none of this is a shortcut to success. That still involves a lot of art. For that matter, it's still hard to get the science right.

What have you learned about developing the art part of the process?

The best founders are artists in their domain. They operate instinctively in their industry because they are in touch with every relevant data point. They're able to synthesize in their gut a tremendous amount of data—pulling together technology trends, their companies' capabilities, their competitors' activities, market psychology, every conceivable aspect of how you run a company. A large number of tech companies that failed did so when they brought in a new CEO and the company stopped innovating and sold out. It's very hard to transplant a founder's skill set to someone coming from the outside.

Are VCs actually any good at finding great companies?

Research shows that there is a very high correlation between the top VC firms and persistent returns. These firms are good at what they do, but we believe that only a very small part of that is because they're smart. It also has to do with the persistence of the deal flow. It's a buyer-driven market for capital. And the best entrepreneurs want to raise money from the top firms, because they want the positive signaling effect—which is especially important for recruiting top talent. As a consequence, most second- or third-tier firms don't have the option of funding great companies. It doesn't matter how good the picker is. He'll never get to see the deal.

You've made some good bets—on Twitter, Facebook, Skype, and others. Is there one bet you missed out on that you wish you hadn't?

Square [an electronic payment service] is our great white whale. We've passed on every single round and we've regretted it pretty much every time. But we're proud of our results so far. Our first fund has returned 2x already, with a lot more companies still to mature— which has allowed us to raise the other funds very quickly.

You've developed a strong philanthropic focus. Is the next generation of investors thinking about social investment?

No. [Laughs.]

So much for my hopes for the next generation.

Many younger entrepreneurs have a social mission or a philanthropic agenda. They start early. Investors, not so much.

Originally published in May 2013. Reprint R1305G

Six Myths About Venture Capitalists

by Diane Mulcahy

STEVE JOBS, MARK ZUCKERBERG, SERGEY BRIN: We celebrate these entrepreneurs for their successes, and often equally extol the venture capitalists who backed their start-ups and share in their glory. Well-known VC firms such as Kleiner Perkins and Sequoia have cultivated a branded mystique around their ability to find and finance the most successful young companies. Forbes identifies the top individual VCs on its Midas List, implicitly crediting them with a mythical magic touch for investing. The story of venture capital appears to be a compelling narrative of bold investments and excess returns.

The reality looks very different. Behind the anecdotes about Apple, Facebook, and Google are numbers showing that many more venture-backed start-ups fail than succeed. And VCs themselves aren't much better at generating returns. For more than a decade the stock markets have outperformed most of them, and since 1999 VC funds on average have barely broken even.

The VC industry wouldn't exist without entrepreneurs, yet entrepreneurs often feel as if they're in the backseat when it comes to dealing with VCs. For someone who's starting (or thinking of starting) a company, the myths surrounding venture capital can be powerful. In this article I will challenge some common ones in order to help company founders develop a more realistic sense of the industry and what it offers.

Myth 1: Venture Capital Is the Primary Source of Start-Up Funding

Venture capital financing is the exception, not the norm, among start-ups. Historically, only a tiny percentage (fewer than 1%) of U.S. companies have raised capital from VCs. And the industry is contracting: After peaking in the late 1990s, the number of active VC firms fell from 744 to 526 in the decade 2001–2011, and the amount of venture capital raised was just under $19 billion in 2011, down from $39 billion in 2001, according to the National Venture Capital Association (NVCA).

But less venture capital doesn't mean less start-up capital. Non-VC sources of financing are growing rapidly and giving entrepreneurs many more choices than in the past. Angel investors—affluent individuals who invest smaller amounts of capital at an earlier stage than VCs do—fund more than 16 times as many companies as VCs do, and their share is growing. In 2011 angels invested more than $22 billion in approximately 65,000 companies, whereas venture capitalists invested about $28 billion in about 3,700 companies. AngelList, an online platform that connects start-ups with angel capital, is one example of the enormous growth in angel financing. Since it launched, in 2010, more than 2,000 companies have raised capital using the platform, and start-ups now raise more than $10 million a month there. (Disclosure: The Kauffman Foundation is an investor in AngelList.)

Another new source of start-up investment is crowdfunding, whereby entrepreneurs raise small amounts of capital from large numbers of people in exchange for nonequity rewards such as products from the newly funded company. Kickstarter reports that more than 18,000 projects raised nearly $320 million through its platform in 2012—triple the amount raised in 2011. Passage of the JOBS (Jumpstart Our Business Startups) Act last year promises to support even faster growth by allowing crowdfunders to invest in exchange for equity and by expanding the pool of investors who can participate.

Idea in Brief

As the director of private equity for the Kauffman Foundation and a former venture capitalist, Mulcahy has observed the industry closely. In 2012 she and two Kauffman colleagues published a report titled "We Have Met the Enemy . . . and He Is Us," based on a comprehensive analysis of the foundation's more than 20 years of experience investing in nearly 100 VC funds. Her research and experience led her to advise aspiring entrepreneurs against falling victim to these common myths about venture capital:

1. It's the primary source of start-up funding. (Actually, angel investors fund 16 times as many companies, and in 2012 more than 18,000 entrepreneurs raised nearly $320 million through a single crowdfunding site.)

2. VCs take big risks with start-ups. (Often they're insulated against risk by hefty annual fee streams.)

3. Most VCs offer great advice and mentoring. (To avoid disappointment on this front, ask the CEOs of other portfolio companies how they'd rate the firm.)

4. VC generates spectacular returns. (Since 1997 less cash has been returned to VC investors than they have invested.)

5. Bigger is better. (Research shows that fund performance declines as fund size increases above $250 million.)

6. VCs are innovators. (Apparently not. The innovation is coming from online platforms such as AngelList and SecondMarket.)

Myth 2: VCs Take a Big Risk When They Invest in Your Start-Up

VCs are often portrayed as risk takers who back bold new ideas. True, they take a lot of risk with their *investors'* capital—but very little with their own. In most VC funds the partners' own money accounts for just 1% of the total. The industry's revenue model, long investment cycle, and lack of visible performance data make VCs less accountable for their performance than most other professional investors. If a VC firm invests in your start-up, it will be rooting for you to succeed. But it will probably do just fine financially even if you fail.

Why? Because the standard VC fund charges an annual fee of 2% on committed capital over the life of the fund—usually 10 years—plus a percentage of the profits when firms successfully exit, usually by being acquired or going public. So a firm that raised a $1 billion fund and charged a 2% fee would receive a fixed fee stream of $20 million *a year* to cover expenses and compensation. VC firms raise new funds about every three or four years, so let's say that three years into the first fund, the firm raised a second $1 billion fund. That would generate an additional $20 million in fees, for a total of $40 million annually. These cumulative and guaranteed management fees insulate VC partners from poor returns because much of their compensation comes from fees. Many partners take home compensation in the seven figures regardless of the fund's investment performance. Most entrepreneurs have no such safety net.

Other investment professionals often face far greater performance pressure. Consider mutual fund managers, whose fund performance is reported daily, whose investors can withdraw money at any time, and who are often replaced for underperformance. VC performance is ultimately judged at the end of a fund's 10-year life, so venture capitalists are free from the level of accountability that's common in other investment realms. They take on less personal risk than angel investors or crowdfunders, who use their own capital. And all investors take fewer risks than most entrepreneurs, who put much of their net worth and all of their earning capacity into their start-ups.

Myth 3: Most VCs Offer Great Advice and Mentoring

A common VC pitch to entrepreneurs is that the firm brings much more than money to the table: It offers experience, operational and industry expertise, a broad network of relevant contacts, a range of services for start-ups, and a strong track record of successful investing.

In some cases those nonmonetary resources really are valuable. But VCs vary tremendously—both as firms and as individuals—in how much effort they put into advising and assisting portfolio companies. Among those who do mentor their CEOs, ability and the quality of advice can differ widely. There are no solid data about the industry's delivery on this mentoring promise. But if you asked the CEOs of 100 VC-funded companies how helpful their VCs are, some would say they're fabulous, some would say they're active but not a huge help, and some would say they do little beyond writing checks. This last group isn't necessarily bad, of course: Some CEOs may be happy to skip the mentoring and just take the cash. But for founders who have bought into the idea that VCs provide lots of value-added help, it can be a source of great disappointment.

The best way to determine whether a VC firm or partner brings resources other than capital to the table is to conduct your own due diligence, just as you'd do a thorough reference check on a key hire. Talk with the CEOs of the firm's other portfolio companies and ask if the partner is accessible, how much he or she adds to boardroom discussion, and whether the CEO has received constructive help in dealing with company problems. Ask about resources the firm offers—PR, recruiting, and so forth—and whether those have been useful.

Some questions you should ask the VC firm directly, such as: Whom does it intend to put on your board? Is the person a partner or an associate? Does the person have any experience (or any other portfolio companies) in your industry? On how many other boards does he or she serve? Asking such questions may seem like common sense, but it's shocking how few company founders actually make the necessary calls before signing up for a long-term relationship with a VC. If part of what makes a firm attractive is that it offers expertise, mentoring, and services, the entrepreneur needs to confirm that both the firm and the partner have a track record of delivering them.

Myth 4: VCs Generate Spectacular Returns

Last year my colleagues at the Kauffman Foundation and I published a widely read report, "We Have Met the Enemy. . . and He Is Us," about the venture capital industry and its returns. We found that the overall performance of the industry is poor. VC funds haven't significantly outperformed the public markets since the late 1990s, and since 1997 less cash has been returned to VC investors than they have invested. A tiny group of top-performing firms do generate great "venture rates of return": at least twice the capital invested, net of fees. We don't know definitively which firms are in that group, because performance data are not generally available and are not consistently reported. The average fund, however, breaks even or loses money.

We analyzed the Kauffman Foundation's experience investing in nearly 100 VC funds over 20 years. We found that only 20 of our funds outperformed the markets by the 3% to 5% annually that we expect to compensate us for the fees and illiquidity we incur by investing in private rather than public equity. Even worse, 62 of our 100 funds failed to beat the returns available from a small-cap public index.

Venture capital investments are generally perceived as high-risk and high-reward. The data in our report reveal that although investors in VC take on high fees, illiquidity, and risk, they rarely reap the reward of high returns. Entrepreneurs who are distressed when VCs decline to fund their ventures need only review the performance data to see that VCs as a group have no Midas touch for investing.

Myth 5: In VC, Bigger Is Better

Venture capital in the United States began as a cottage industry, notable in the early years for investments in companies such as Intel, Microsoft, and Apple. In 1990, 100 VC firms were actively investing, with slightly less than $30 billion under management, according to the NVCA. During that era venture capital generated strong, above-market returns, and performance by any measure was good. What happened? During the peak of the internet boom, in 2000, the number of active firms grew to more than 1,000, and assets under management exceeded $220 billion. VC didn't scale well. As in most asset classes, when the money flooded in, returns fell, and venture capital has not yet recovered. The number of firms and the amount of capital have declined since the boom, though they are both still far above the levels of the early and middle 1990s.

What's true for the industry is also true for individual funds: Bigger isn't better. Company founders often feel that signing a deal with a large VC firm lends cachet, just as MBA students may get special pleasure from being offered a job by a big, well-known employer. But industry and academic studies show that fund performance declines as fund size increases above $250 million. We found that the VC funds larger than $400 million in Kauffman's portfolio generally failed to provide attractive returns: Just four out of 30 outperformed a publicly traded small-cap index fund.

Myth 6: VCs Are Innovators

It's ironic that VC firms position themselves as supporters, financers, and even instigators of innovation, yet the industry itself has been devoid of innovation for the past 20 years. Venture capital has seen plenty of changes over time—more funds, more money, bigger funds, declining returns—but funds are structured, capital is raised, and partners are paid just as they were two decades ago. Any innovation in financing start-ups, such as crowdfunding and platforms like AngelList and SecondMarket, has come from outside the VC industry.

The story of venture capital is changing. Entrepreneurs have more choices for financing their companies, shifting the historical balance of power that has too long tilted too far toward VCs. Entrepreneurs will enjoy a different view as they move from the backseat into the driver's seat in negotiating with VCs. An emerging group of "VC 2.0" firms are going back to raising small funds and focusing on generating great returns rather than large fees. And the industry's persistent underperformance is finally causing institutional investors to think twice before investing in venture capital. As a result, VCs will continue to play a significant, but most likely smaller, role in channeling capital to disruptive start-ups.

Originally published in May 2013. Reprint R1305E

Chobani's Founder on Growing a Start-Up Without Outside Investors

by Hamdi Ulukaya

I'VE ALWAYS LOVED YOGURT—the thick kind I grew up eating in Turkey, where my mother made it from scratch on our family's dairy farm. When I moved to the United States, in 1994, I found American yogurt to be disgusting—too sugary and watery. If I wanted yogurt, I usually made it myself at home. So when I came across a piece of junk mail advertising a fully equipped yogurt factory for sale, in March 2005, I was curious. The factory was about 65 miles west of the feta cheese company, Euphrates, that I'd started in upstate New York a few years earlier. In 2005 Euphrates had fewer than 40 employees and about $2 million in sales; it was barely breaking even.

Kraft owned the yogurt factory, and it had decided to get out of the yogurt business. The advertisement showed some photographs of the building, which had been constructed in 1920 and appeared to be in rough shape. On a whim, I called the broker and arranged to drive over the next morning to take a look.

The factory was a sad place, sort of like a cemetery, in a very small town. Fifty-five employees were preparing to shut it down. A lot of equipment was included, but it was old. The best thing about

Creating a Market, One Container at a Time

2005

Hamdi Ulukaya buys an old Kraft yogurt plant in upstate New York.

2006

The plant makes U.S.-style yogurt for other companies, while Ulukaya and a Turkish-born yogurt maker develop the Chobani recipe.

2007

The first cup of Chobani hits grocery shelves in Great Neck, New York.

2009

Chobani becomes the best-selling brand of Greek yogurt in the United States.

2010

Chobani becomes the best-selling brand of all yogurt in the United States and expands to Canada and Australia.

2013

Chobani sales are expected to top $1.3 billion.

---

the place was the price: less than $1 million. Some of the individual machines would cost more than that if purchased new.

On the drive home I called my attorney, who is my main business adviser. I told him I wanted to buy the factory. He thought it was a terrible idea. He had three good arguments: First, because I'd be buying it "as is," I really had no idea how well it would function. Second, Kraft is a pretty successful company, and if it was giving up on this facility, this town, and the yogurt industry, maybe it knew something I didn't. Third, and maybe the strongest objection, where was I going to get that kind of money? He was right: At that point, I had nowhere near enough money for such a big purchase.

But as it turned out, I was able to borrow the money to buy the factory—and after Chobani hit the market, I financed our growth through further bank loans and reinvested profits. This is a crucial piece of the Chobani story. Our ability to grow without reliance on external investors—the venture capitalists, private equity types, strategic partners, and potential acquirers who've offered us money

Idea in Brief

The author grew up on a dairy farm in Turkey, where his mother made yogurt from scratch. When he moved to the United States, in 1994, he found the yogurt to be "disgusting—too sugary and watery." So he made his own at home.

By 2005 he was running a cheese factory in upstate New York when he saw an ad for a run-down but fully equipped yogurt factory that Kraft was divesting. It had a price tag below $1 million. Against the advice of his attorney and business adviser, he bought the factory with a bank loan backed by the Small Business Administration and immediately hired a master yogurt maker from Turkey. They spent two years perfecting their recipe, and

Ulukaya worked hard to get the packaging just right.

Three crucial decisions allowed him to finance growth after the business took off: He insisted that Chobani be sold in mainstream grocery stores and be stocked in the dairy aisle alongside existing yogurt brands. He negotiated with retailers over their slotting fees. And he spent a lot of time determining the right unit selling price.

Within a few weeks of launch, very large orders started coming in; by 2009 the company was selling 200,000 cases of yogurt a week. It needed to make a big investment to increase capacity—but Ulukaya ruled out private equity investors. Here he tells why.

since we launched—was vital to our success. Today Chobani is a $1 billion business, and I remain the sole owner. That means I can run the company the way I choose—and plan for its future without pressure from outsiders.

Too many entrepreneurs believe it's impossible to scale a business without relying on VCs or other equity investors. That view is wrong. If I could grow a company from zero to $1 billion in less than a decade in a capital-intensive industry, many other businesses can too.

Slotting Our Cups

To buy the yogurt factory, I obtained a bank loan backed by the U.S. Small Business Administration. I learned about SBA loans from two loan officers at KeyBank. I spent two days writing a business plan, offered a personal guarantee, and put up 10% of the purchase price. The bank and the government put up the other 90%, with a low interest rate and a 10-year term. The loan was sufficient to create a small amount of working capital in addition to the purchase price. The process took about five months, and on August 17, 2005, I had the keys to the factory.

I immediately hired a master yogurt maker from Turkey, and we spent the next two years perfecting our recipe. I hired four employees who'd worked at the Kraft plant, and because we had nothing to produce, I kept them busy repainting and repairing the factory for a few months. By early 2006 we'd begun making private-label American-style yogurt as a contract manufacturer for other companies, just to bring in some revenue.

In addition to fine-tuning our own recipe, we worked hard to get the packaging right. This was a big expense—about $250,000. American yogurt has always been sold in containers with relatively narrow openings. In Europe yogurt containers are wider and squatter, and that's what I wanted for Chobani—I wanted the package to signal that the product inside was very different.

By late 2007 we were ready to go to market. At that point we made several crucial decisions that allowed us to finance our growth once the business took off.

First, we insisted that Chobani be sold in mainstream grocery stores rather than specialty stores, and that it be stocked in the dairy aisle, alongside existing yogurt brands, rather than in the gourmet or natural food aisles. That's probably the single most important decision we made. Although many Americans had never heard of Greek yogurt until Chobani launched, at least one rival brand had been selling Greek yogurt in specialty stores since the mid-1990s. But because it had limited distribution, it remained a tiny niche product. We wanted Chobani to be accessible to everyone. If we'd said yes to early offers from specialty stores, the company never would have grown as quickly as it did.

Second, we negotiated with retailers over their slotting fees. Most big supermarkets were asking a minimum of $10,000 per SKU to stock our product, and some were asking up to $100,000, so if we wanted to put six flavors of yogurt in a store, it would want an up-front payment of at least $60,000. We didn't have that kind of money. So we negotiated to pay off the slotting fees over time as the yogurt sold.

Third, I worked really hard to determine the right unit selling price to fund future growth. I spent a lot of time figuring out our cup costs, ingredient costs, and labor costs, and I made a simple model to calculate the exact price that would allow us to break even once we hit 20,000 cases a week in sales. That's a relatively low volume: It meant that if customers liked the product, we'd quickly be profitable and could re-invest our profits in growth. We ended up charging less than $1.50 a cup—more than traditional American brands (which typically sold for less than $1), but far less than the European-style yogurt that sold for $3 to $5 in gourmet stores. A lot of new companies would have launched at a lower price and tried to raise the price later. I avoided that by figuring out an initial price that made long-term sense.

Often when a start-up launches a product, there's an agonizing wait to see if customers will buy it. We didn't have that problem. Within a couple of weeks after Chobani got into ShopRite, we started getting orders for 5,000 cases. The first time we received one, I kept double-checking to make sure it didn't say 500. It quickly became clear that our biggest challenge wasn't going to be selling enough yogurt—it was going to be making enough yogurt.

Over the next 18 months we found ways to increase the capacity of our factory without making big investments. We couldn't afford new equipment, so we went around the country to find used equipment and arranged to buy it on installment. Eventually we retrofitted our filling machine—the big constraint on our plant—so that it could handle 100,000 cases a week. We also limited our capital investment by relying on manual labor instead of automation: For instance, the finished cups of yogurt were hand-packed in cartons. During that time I rarely left the factory—I slept there most nights.

We were extremely careful with cash. Too many start-ups hire people in anticipation of growth; we waited until the business was bigger. Every Friday I met with our finance guy. I made sure that our employees and our milk suppliers were paid on time, but we let a lot of other bills go a little longer. Because we had set up the business to be profitable early, every cup of yogurt we sold gave us more free cash. Our model had other advantages: Yogurt is perishable, which limits inventories; and supermarkets pay us promptly after delivery, whereas most of our suppliers give us a month or two to pay. That really helped our cash flow.

Sticking to the Mission

A few months after our first sale, I began getting calls from potential investors. In early 2008 we attended a convention in Anaheim called Expo West, where natural products manufacturers meet buyers from big retail chains. The show attracts a lot of investors, and we were repeatedly approached by people who said they'd like a stake in Chobani. Most of them said we would need much more cash if we really wanted to grow. They also said we'd benefit from having experienced managers and strategists aboard, to help us figure out how to navigate as we grew larger.

This was all new to me. I didn't even know what private equity was. I was running Chobani as a simple mom-and-pop operation. I had no strategy for dealing with potential investors. But Greek yogurt was becoming so popular that bigger players such as Dannon and Yoplait were going to launch their own versions. We needed to grow quickly enough to prevent established companies from stealing the market we'd created. So it felt like the race was on.

For a while I took calls and meetings with private equity firms. It was a learning process. They try to make you doubt yourself—it's a standard part of their pitch. I kept hearing the same things over and over: "You've never done this before." "This is not a world for a start-up." They talked about the size of the marketing budget I'd need when Dannon came in. They emphasized the experience and sophistication and knowledge they'd bring to my business.

But the more I thought about it, the more confident I grew. We didn't have experience, but most of our early decisions had been right. The product and packaging were really good. We'd gotten our product into the dairy aisle when experienced people said it belonged in the natural foods section. And the word of mouth was so strong that marketing was taking care of itself. Besides money, what exactly would these people bring to the table?

One reason I could have that attitude is that Chobani's quick success had made our bankers willing to fund our growth. In 2009 we needed to make a big investment to boost our capacity. We were selling 200,000 cases a week, and I wanted to increase that to one million cases. We'd need at least $30 million in new loans. By then our bankers had been watching us for four years, and they'd seen growing profitability over the previous 18 months. Our growth projections were based on simple math: We were still selling mostly in the Northeast, and if supermarkets in the rest of the country sold as much Chobani as our existing accounts did, the demand would easily justify our expansion plans.

I also knew that as soon as I took money from investors, the clock would start ticking. Private equity investors want to cash out in five to seven years—they would probably push us to sell Chobani to a big

Creating a category

Since Chobani's launch, Greek yogurt has stolen share from traditional yogurt—but it has also helped grow the overall U.S. yogurt market by more than $1 billion.

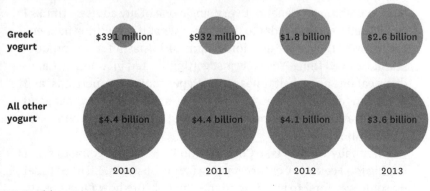

	2010	2011	2012	2013
Greek yogurt	$391 million	$932 million	$1.8 billion	$2.6 billion
All other yogurt	$4.4 billion	$4.4 billion	$4.1 billion	$3.6 billion

Source: Nielsen

food company. I've seen other small food companies go that route, and inevitably they lose their souls. I care about the integrity of our product—I want it to be delicious, nutritious, and accessible to everyone. If I took on investors, my ability to stick to this mission would be limited. I had spent two years living in that factory; it was working now, and it was my baby. Eventually I simply stopped returning calls from potential investors. There really wasn't anything to talk about.

Bigger competitors did bring their own Greek yogurts to market, but much more slowly than I'd expected. When I first tasted one of them, it was so terrible I thought it must have spoiled. I sent someone out to buy a few more cups, but they all tasted the same. I even wondered whether the company might deliberately be making its Greek yogurt taste terrible in an attempt to turn off consumers and spoil the entire category in order to preserve the profits of its established brands of sugary yogurt. I had put aside $7 million for a big ad campaign when our larger rivals launched their Greek yogurts, but after I tasted their products, I canceled the ads. There was no need.

Today we have a syndicate of banks and a credit line to meet our capital requirements. In December 2012 we opened a factory in Idaho, and altogether we've invested about $700 million in our plants and equipment. Today we produce more than 2 million cases of yogurt a week, and our business is still growing.

The biggest downside of our self-financing approach is that nearly 100% of my net worth is in Chobani. To financial planners, that's a nightmare scenario. Every single one of my advisers thinks I should sell a stake in order to diversify. "What if something happens tomorrow?" they say. But I don't think enthusiasm for our product is a short-lived thing. Yogurt is just getting started in America. Canadians eat one and a half times as much per capita as Americans, and Europeans eat up to seven and a half times as much. Now that good yogurt is available here, people are eating more. Foodies and chefs and nutritionists love it.

Eventually we may take Chobani public. If I'm not going to sell it to a big food company or turn it into a family business, I'll need to set up some way for it to live beyond me. I'm not sure how I'll choose to turn Chobani into a legacy—but that's a nice problem to have.

Editors' Note

In 2012 Ulukaya was sued by his ex-wife, Ayse Giray, who claims that money she invested in his feta cheese business in the early 2000s provided the initial financing for Chobani. She is seeking a 53% stake in Chobani. The company says Ulukaya has always been and remains the sole shareholder of Chobani, and no shares of the cheese business have ever been issued to any outside investors.

Originally published in October 2013. Reprint R1310A

Network Effects Aren't Enough

by Andrei Hagiu and Simon Rothman

IN MANY WAYS, ONLINE MARKETPLACES are the perfect business model. Since they just facilitate transactions between suppliers and customers rather than take possession of or full responsibility for products or services, they have very low cost structures and very high gross margins—70% for eBay, 60% for Etsy. And network effects make them highly defensible. Alibaba, Craigslist, eBay, and Rakuten are more than 15 years old, but they still dominate their sectors.

Little wonder that entrepreneurs and investors are rushing to build the next eBay or Airbnb or Uber for every imaginable product and service category. In the past 10 years, the number of marketplaces worth more than $1 billion has gone from two—Craigslist and eBay—to more than a dozen in the United States, including Airbnb, Etsy, Groupon, GrubHub Seamless, Lending Club, Lyft, Prosper, Thumbtack, Uber, and Upwork. And that number is expected to double by 2020, according to Greylock Partners, a Silicon Valley venture capital firm where one of us (Simon) is a partner.

Yet online marketplaces remain extremely difficult to build. Most entrepreneurs see it as a chicken-and-egg problem: To attain a critical mass of buyers, you need a critical mass of suppliers—but to attract suppliers, you need a lot of buyers. This challenge does indeed trip up many marketplaces. But even after a marketplace has attracted a critical mass of both buyers and sellers, it's far from smooth sailing. Our combined experience in evaluating, advising, and investing in hundreds of marketplace businesses (including several mentioned in this article) suggests that other pitfalls can derail marketplaces: growing too fast too early; fostering insufficient trust and safety; resorting to sticks rather than carrots to deter user disintermediation; and regulatory risk. In this article, we discuss how to avoid those hazards.

Growth

Once marketplaces reach a critical inflection point, network effects kick in and growth follows an exponential, rather than linear, trajectory. These network effects also create barriers to entry: Once many buyers and sellers are using a marketplace, it becomes harder for a rival to lure them away. As a result, entrepreneurs often mistakenly assume that they need to reach the exponential growth phase as quickly as possible. But a headlong rush to fast growth is often unnecessary and can even backfire, for several reasons.

The importance of first-mover advantage for marketplaces is overstated

Entrepreneurs should really focus on being the first to create a *liquid market* in their segment. The winning marketplace is the first one to figure out how to enable mutually beneficial transactions between suppliers and buyers—not the first one out of the gate. Indeed, many prominent marketplaces were not first movers: Airbnb was founded more than a decade after VRBO; Alibaba was a second mover in China after eBay; and Uber's UberX copied Lyft's peer-to-peer taxi business model.

Why does being the first mover provide less of an advantage than is commonly assumed? The reason is that chasing early growth before a marketplace has proved its value to both buyers and sellers leaves the business vulnerable to competition from later entrants. If either side's users do not derive significant value on a consistent basis, they will readily jump ship. But when buyers have access to a sufficient selection of products or services at attractive prices and sellers earn attractive profits, neither side has an incentive to go

Idea in Brief

The Misconception

Most entrepreneurs believe that the key challenge in building online marketplaces is to attract a critical mass of buyers and sellers. But before or even after that hurdle has been overcome, there are others looming that can hurt, if not kill, these businesses.

Overlooked Challenges

Growing too quickly can exacerbate the flaws that are inevitable in any business model. Common approaches for establishing trust and safety rarely work on their own. Using sticks rather than carrots to deter disintermediation can backfire. And regulatory issues can derail a promising business.

The Solution

Before scaling, marketplaces must lay out a compelling value proposition for buyers and sellers. They need to build trust and create incentives to keep them on the platform. And they need to engage regulators as soon as their buyer-seller proposition is clear.

elsewhere, and strong network effects kick in rapidly: More buyers bring more sellers and vice versa.

Groupon and LivingSocial—platforms where retailers sell discounted offerings to consumers—provide a cautionary tale. Both companies expanded aggressively, attracting millions of users and thousands of merchants. Their success, however, was short-lived: Once merchants realized that Groupon and LivingSocial discounts did not bring repeat customers, they began to do business on many competing deal sites. As a result, Groupon's value fell from $18 billion at the time of its 2011 IPO to less than $2 billion today; LivingSocial filed for an IPO at $10 billion in 2011, withdrew, and was acquired by Amazon. By the end of 2014, it was worth less than $250 million.

Growing too early puts stress on the business model

A start-up's initial business model inevitably has flaws that must be fixed. But because growth for marketplaces can be so explosive, it puts much more pressure on the business model than does the more linear growth experienced by regular product or service firms, amplifying the impact of the flaws and making them harder to fix. Indeed, trying to change the model while growing very fast increases

Airbnb's remarkable growth

It didn't take long for Airbnb to surpass conventional hotel chains in the number of rooms available worldwide to travelers. Its explosive growth and huge market cap are testaments to the outsize potential of online marketplaces.

Company	Number of rooms	Founded	Market cap	Time to 1M rooms	Real estate assets
Airbnb	1M+	2008	$25B	7 yrs	$0
Marriott	1.1M	1957	$16B	58 yrs	$985M
Hilton	745k	1919	$19B	N/A	$9.1B
Intercontinental Hotel Group	727k	1988	$9B	N/A	$741M

Source: Reuters, Marriott, Intercontinental Hotels Group, Wikipedia, New York Times, BAMSEC. Data as of end of 2015

the risk of a catastrophic breakdown. Thus, premature growth can actually reduce the probability of reaching the inflection point that triggers exponential growth.

For these reasons, marketplace entrepreneurs should resist the temptation to accelerate growth before figuring out an optimal *supply-demand fit*—that is, when buyers are as happy to purchase the products or services as providers are to supply them. This may mean waiting much longer than conventional companies do to scale a new offering. For example, Airbnb took two years to figure out exactly how to allow individuals to rent their homes to complete strangers under conditions and at prices that satisfied both parties. (Recall that the initial service was an air mattress and a cooked breakfast. In most cases, this was either not what travelers wanted or not something hosts were willing to offer.)

The wrong type of growth can hurt performance

Many marketplaces find it tempting to grow through "power sellers"—those who have moved from selling as a hobby or source of supplemental income to running a full-time business on the marketplace. That's because attracting a few power sellers is more cost-effective than attracting many nonprofessional sellers, and the former tend to be more efficient at carrying out transactions than the latter.

However, growth through power sellers can be undesirable. After building most of its early growth on power sellers, eBay discovered that their dominance forced it to make compromises that favored those sellers but hurt the buyer experience. For example, power sellers demanded the ability to do "bulk listings" (to automate the listing of many products), which was more efficient from the sellers' point of view. This created problems for eBay: By skewing seller incentives toward commodity goods, bulk listings reduced the diversity of products offered for sale, crowding out unique products and causing the quality of the average listing to go down. Furthermore, bulk listings enabled power sellers to negotiate lower per-listing fees from eBay. Over the years, power sellers came to dominate eBay's supply side and made it difficult for nonprofessional sellers to compete.

Other types of marketplaces face a similar issue. In the case of Airbnb, multi-property hosts might show pictures of certain apartments on the site but switch travelers to different ones upon arrival to suit the hosts' planning needs. Or hosts that bought property specifically to list on the site might not provide the authentic experience that travelers seek. As a result, Airbnb may have to place some limits on multi-property hosts, even though that would conceivably negatively impact growth in the short run.

The bottom line: Platforms should resist the temptation to use the industrialization of the supply side to boost growth.

Trust and Safety

By definition, an online marketplace does not directly control the quality of the products or services that are bought and sold on its platform, so it must put mechanisms in place to ensure that participants have little or no fear about conducting business on the site. The goal is to eliminate (or at least minimize) improper behavior, such as abusing rented property, misrepresenting products, and outright fraud.

Ratings-and-reviews systems have been the most widely used mechanism for engendering trust between marketplace participants ever since eBay's first successful large-scale implementation of such a system, in 1998. Nearly all prominent marketplaces use R&R systems, which typically allow the two sides of the market to rate and review each other by awarding stars (1 to 5), providing text feedback, or both.

However, research shows that these systems rarely build sufficient trust or provide adequate safety on their own. Many online R&R systems suffer from significant biases: People who voluntarily rate a product or service tend to be either very happy or very unhappy with it. This severely undermines the value of the information provided and skews results.

For instance, a recent study estimated that more than 50% of eBay sellers have received positive feedback for 100% of the transactions rated by their buyers, and 90% of sellers have received positive feedback for more than 98% of the transactions rated by their buyers. There are several reasons for this. Many buyers want to be nice, so they leave exceedingly generous reviews. Some fear that sellers will harass them by e-mail if they leave negative feedback. Many unhappy buyers simply leave and do not return to the site. And a few take extreme (and comical) measures: A good example of an R&R system gone awry is the phenomenon of sarcastic reviews on Amazon's marketplace. Fake reviewers take over the comments for a product or service, awarding 4 or 5 stars and then writing ironically scathing, often hilarious comments.

Even reliable ratings and reviews systems are not enough to overcome potential users' fears that something bad might happen, especially when the stakes are high. It's hard to imagine buying or renting cars or houses from complete strangers solely on the basis of positive user reviews. And when things go wrong, users often hold the marketplace at least partly responsible, even though technically it is merely an enabler of transactions. A buyer who has a bad experience may blame the corresponding seller and leave a bad review, but he or she may also blame the marketplace and never return, which hurts all other sellers.

To properly engender trust and overcome fears, marketplaces must go beyond R&R systems and accept some de facto responsibility for transactions. This can take several forms:

Provide insurance to one or both parties in a transaction

Turo (formerly RelayRides), a marketplace where individuals can rent their cars to other people, offers specially designed insurance policies that provide coverage to both parties. Airbnb now insures hosts against property damage of up to $1 million. Lyft and Uber provide insurance coverage to their drivers for damage done to others.

Vet and certify participants

Upwork (formerly Elance-oDesk) has developed hundreds of proprietary certification tests that it administers to freelance contractors on its platform to assure buyers that the workers they hire are qualified.

Offer dispute resolution and payment security services

Airbnb holds the money paid by the traveler in escrow for 24 hours after the traveler has checked in; Alibaba holds the money paid by the buyer in escrow until the buyer confirms receipt of the goods from the seller. And both Airbnb and Alibaba have comprehensive dispute resolution procedures that offer recourse to both sides of the market.

Disintermediation

Many marketplaces fear that once they facilitate a successful transaction, the buyer and the seller will agree to conduct their subsequent interactions outside the marketplace. This risk is greatest for marketplaces that handle high-value transactions (eBay Motors, Beepi) or recurring transactions (Airbnb, CoachUp, Handy, Hourly-Nerd, Upwork). But in our experience, entrepreneurs tend to overestimate the threat of disintermediation and choose the wrong approach to prevent it.

The instinct is often to impose penalties, such as temporarily suspending accounts, if attempts to take transactions off a platform are detected. The fact of the matter is that all marketplaces that facilitate high-value or recurring transactions suffer some disintermediation: Some hosts and guests take their transactions off Airbnb, as do some contractors and employers that first connected on Upwork. But we have yet to see a promising marketplace that has been severely hindered—let alone put out of business—by this behavior, and we've found that carrots are more effective deterrents than sticks. For example, algorithms for detecting transactions initiated online but completed offline are difficult and costly to implement and can create user resentment.

Participants usually prefer to conduct business in a "well-lit showroom" that reduces search or transaction costs and allows deals to be conducted securely and comfortably. As long as a marketplace provides value, there should be sufficient incentive for one or both sides to conduct all their transactions through the platform. If users find it onerous to do so, then either the marketplace does not create enough value or its fees are too high.

One company that has successful incentives to combat disintermediation is eBay Motors. It provides an automatic purchase-protection service against certain types of fraud (for example, nondelivery of the vehicle), facilitates car inspections through partner shops at discounted rates, and uses its bargaining power to help sellers obtain lower shipping costs. Another example is Upwork. In addition to providing worker certifications, it allows employers to audit and monitor the work being done by contractors in real time. It also allows them to process online payments in many currencies at discounted exchange fees. As these examples show, some of the mechanisms that make transactions safer to conduct also help reduce the risk of disintermediation, killing two birds with one stone.

Regulation

Online marketplaces that provide radically new alternatives to conventional business models test the limits of existing regulatory frameworks almost by definition. They enable new types of transactions, such as peer-to-peer lending or property rentals. As a result, marketplaces face serious regulatory challenges much more frequently than traditional product or service companies do. Should homeowners renting out their properties be subject to hotel taxes? Under what conditions should individuals be allowed to sell rides in their cars? When should marketplaces for services be allowed to treat their service providers as independent contractors and when should they be compelled to treat them as employees?

With respect to regulatory risks, most entrepreneurs have one of two reflexes: ignore them or try to fix everything up front. Neither is a good idea. Unwinding a regulatory problem late tends to be much more difficult than preventing it early. Furthermore, ignoring regulations can generate bad press, which may alienate users. At the other extreme, attempting to clear all regulatory hurdles from the beginning is unrealistic. Regulatory time frames are too long for most young companies to work within, and it is very hard to gain clearance for a business concept that has not yet been proved in the market. (For a look at this problem from the incumbent's perspective, see "Spontaneous Deregulation," by Benjamin Edelman and Damien Geradin, in the April 2016 issue of HBR.)

The right approach, not surprisingly, is somewhere in the middle: Strive to engage regulators without breaking stride or slowing down to the decision-making speed of governments. No marketplace we know of has dealt with all its regulatory challenges perfectly, but four interconnected guiding principles—developed by David Hantman, Airbnb's former head of global public policy—can help.

1. Define yourself before your opposition or the media does

Marketplace entrepreneurs should develop a clear vision of their business model and find the most positive—yet accurate—way to describe it to the outside world. Then they should engage regulators and the media to ensure that they are understood on their own terms.

2. Pick the time and place to engage with regulators

Entrepreneurs operating in industries subject to heavy and national regulation should consult an industry attorney before launch in order to fully understand all relevant laws. As soon as their buyer-seller proposition is clear, they should initiate a dialogue with regulators in order to obtain either explicit legal clearance (ideal) or an implicit safe haven (second best) for continuing to develop the service.

The examples of Lending Club and Prosper, the two leading peer-to-peer lending marketplaces in the United States, illustrate the importance of smoothing regulatory frictions before they grind you to a halt. Prosper was launched first, in 2005, followed by Lending Club a year later. Lending Club, however, was first to tackle the difficult regulatory issues. Less than two years after its launch, it established a partnership with an FDIC-insured bank so that the loans it facilitated were subject to the same borrower protection, fair lending, and disclosure regulations as regular bank loans. In early 2008, it became the first peer-to-peer lending marketplace to voluntarily go through a quiet period during which it did not accept any new lenders and focused on completing its registration with the U.S. Securities and Exchange Commission (SEC) as an issuer of public investment products.

In contrast, Prosper ignored regulatory issues until scrutiny by the SEC forced it, too, to enter a quiet period. The results of these differing approaches were significant: Prosper's quiet period lasted nine months, whereas Lending Club's lasted just six. And Lending Club was allowed to continue to serve the borrower side of its marketplace during its quiet period; Prosper had to shut down both the investor and the borrower sides. Lending Club eventually overtook Prosper to become the largest peer-to-peer lending marketplace: In 2012, it made $718 million in loans, compared with $153 million for Prosper.

At the other end of the spectrum, marketplaces operating in spaces that are regulated lightly and only at the city or state level can afford to wait until they reach supply-demand fit in their first city before engaging with regulators. While regulatory issues at the national level are usually a matter of life and death for companies, local regulators are typically less powerful and can be more easily circumvented if necessary.

3. Don't just say no; offer constructive ideas
When confronted with regulatory gray areas—an all-too-common occurrence—marketplace entrepreneurs have an opportunity to turn

a potentially adversarial relationship with regulators into a partnership. For example, Getaround, the peer-to-peer car rental platform, preempted a collision by working directly with the California state government to enact a law that allows private individuals to rent out their cars to strangers under separate insurance coverage designed for this purpose. Getaround's approach is remarkable because peer-to-peer car rentals were not explicitly illegal beforehand—meaning that the company incurred a significant risk by drawing regulatory attention to its service.

Even when existing regulations are merely inconvenient for new marketplaces, entrepreneurs should resist the temptation to ignore or thumb their noses at the relevant authorities and strive instead to find an area where their interests align. For example, a major concern for governmental bodies that regulate taxis is ensuring the safety of passengers and drivers. Ridesharing companies should want the same thing. The marketplaces could use their data on driver and passenger identity and on trip times and paths to work constructively with state regulators to create a safer environment than traditional taxi companies provide.

4. Speak softly and carry a big stick

Entrepreneurs should avoid engaging in acrimonious disputes with regulators; at the same time, they should have effective weapons at their disposal to defend their position. They can use two means of leverage when fighting potentially adverse regulation. The first is the power of satisfied buyers and sellers, who are voters and taxpayers likely to resent government interference with a service they value. To harness the support of users, companies should develop a credible infrastructure for running lobbying campaigns in their own behalf: social media, dedicated websites, and so on. For example, Airbnb helped its San Francisco hosts organize rallies around city hall and testify in public hearings, which eventually swayed the city's regulators to legalize short-term rentals in people's homes in 2014 (the "Airbnb law").

The second lever is tax revenue. Marketplaces that generate sizable revenues for local governments have some leverage in regulatory negotiations. For instance, as part of its ongoing efforts to persuade city governments to legalize its service, Airbnb has offered to collect hotel taxes from its hosts and remit them to local authorities in several cities worldwide. This offer, still pending approval, is clearly a powerful negotiating instrument: According to conservative estimates, the taxable revenue generated by Airbnb hosts was more than $5 billion in 2015. This is an interesting case, since few marketplaces have proactively offered to take responsibility for ensuring that their users pay taxes.

Sometimes, if regulatory uncertainty is unlikely to be resolved in the immediate future (a time frame measured in months for start-ups) and the repercussions of noncompliance are severe, then the right response is to comply with the worst-case scenario, even if that means incurring higher costs. One of the most serious regulatory issues now faced by service marketplaces concerns the legal status of their workers. Several prominent service marketplaces (Handy, Lyft, Postmates, Uber, and Washio) are currently contending with class-action lawsuits that accuse them of improperly classifying their workers as independent contractors rather than employees. The cost implications are substantial: Changing a worker's status from independent contractor to employee increases costs by 25% to 40%. While the outcomes of the lawsuits and the corresponding regulation are still uncertain, some marketplace start-ups, including Alfred, Enjoy Technology, Luxe, and Managed by Q, have preempted the issue by voluntarily turning their workers into employees. Early stage start-ups that simply cannot afford to operate under uncertain regulatory status may need to do the same. In most cases, however, an intermediate status somewhere between employee and independent contractor would be the ideal approach.

Online marketplaces are profoundly changing the nature of work and of companies. Since the early days when marketplaces made it possible to sell and buy simple products like PEZ dispensers and handicrafts, the assortment and price range of goods available online has exponentially increased. Over the past five years, platforms for a remarkable variety of task-oriented services have arisen. New technologies such as 3-D printing and virtual reality will continue to open up opportunities for individuals and small firms to directly sell increasingly complex products and services previously provided only by large firms.

The growing number of products and services available through online marketplaces will cause traditional corporate structures to gradually shrink and coexist with overlapping networks of independent workers who come together for limited periods of time to perform specific tasks. The result will be a much more fluid and flexible work environment that empowers both workers and customers. But the challenges of managing growth, building trust and providing safety, minimizing disintermediation, and shaping regulation won't go away. The solution is not to follow the pack. It is to deeply understand the needs of customers, regulators, and society as a whole and, in a disciplined fashion, become an active player in shaping the future.

Originally published in April 2016. Reprint R1604D

Blitzscaling

An interview with Reid Hoffman. **by Tim Sullivan**

REID HOFFMAN IS ONE OF SILICON Valley's grown-ups. After helping to found PayPal, he moved on to found LinkedIn, in 2002, which has turned him into a billionaire. He was an early investor in Facebook and now serves as a partner at the venture capital firm Greylock. He's written two books, *The Start-Up of You* (with Ben Casnocha) and *The Alliance: Managing Talent in the Networked Age* (with Casnocha and Chris Yeh).

In the fall of 2015, Hoffman began teaching a computer science class called Technology-Enabled Blitzscaling at Stanford University, his alma mater, with John Lilly (a partner at Greylock and formerly the CEO of Mozilla), Allen Blue (cofounder of LinkedIn), and Chris Yeh (cofounder of Allied Talent). In this edited interview with Tim Sullivan, the editorial director of HBR Press, Hoffman talks about the challenges, risks, and payoffs of blitzscaling.

HBR: *Let's start with the basics. What is blitzscaling?*

Hoffman: Blitzscaling is what you do when you need to grow really, really quickly. It's the science and art of rapidly building out a company to serve a large and usually global market, with the goal of becoming the first mover at scale.

This is high-impact entrepreneurship. These kinds of companies always create a lot of the jobs and industries of the future. For example, Amazon essentially invented e-commerce. Today, it has over 150,000 employees and has created countless jobs at Amazon sellers and partners. Google revolutionized how we find information—it has over 60,000 employees and has created many more jobs at its AdWords and AdSense partners.

Why this focus on fast growth?

We're in a networked age. And I don't mean only the internet. Globalization is a form of network. It adds networks of transport, commerce, payment, and information flows around the world. In such an environment, you have to move faster, because competition from anywhere on the globe may beat you to scale.

Software has a natural affinity with blitzscaling, because the marginal costs of serving any size market are virtually zero. The more that software becomes integral to all industries, the faster things will move. Throw in AI machine learning, and the loops get even faster. So we're going to see more blitzscaling. Not just a little more, but a lot more.

How did you settle on the term "blitzscaling"? It has some interesting associations.

I have obvious hesitations about the World War II association with the term "blitzkrieg." However, the intellectual parallels are so close that it is very informative. Before blitzkrieg emerged as a military tactic, armies didn't advance beyond their supply lines, which limited their speed. The theory of the blitzkrieg was that if you carried only what you absolutely needed, you could move very, very fast, surprise your enemies, and win. Once you got halfway to your destination, you had to decide whether to turn back or to abandon the lines and go on. Once you made the decision to move forward, you were all in. You won big or lost big.

Blitzscaling adopts a similar perspective. If a start-up determines that it needs to move very fast, it will take on far more risk than a company going through the normal, rational process of scaling up.

This kind of speed is necessary for offensive and defensive reasons. Offensively, your business may require a certain scale to be valuable. LinkedIn wasn't valuable until millions of people joined our network. Marketplaces like eBay must have both buyers and sellers at scale. Payment businesses like PayPal and e-commerce businesses like Amazon have low margins, so they require very high

Idea in Brief

Reid Hoffman is one of Silicon Valley's grown-ups. After helping to found PayPal, he moved on to launch LinkedIn in 2002—an endeavor that turned him into a billionaire. He was an early investor in Facebook and now serves as a partner at the venture capital firm Greylock.

In this edited interview with Tim Sullivan, of HBR Press, Hoffman explores his idea of "blitzscaling"—the discipline of getting very big very fast. In today's networked landscape, the path to high-growth, high-impact entrepreneurship can be chaotic and grueling. It involves rapidly building out a company to serve a large and usually global market, with the goal of becoming the first mover at scale.

And there's no playbook to guide you, Hoffman notes. "You throw yourself off a cliff and assemble your airplane on the way down."

Hoffman emphasizes that blitzscaling is not just about growing revenues and the customer base but also about scaling the organization. People naturally focus on the first two, and "if you don't get those right, then nothing else matters." But very few businesses can succeed on those fronts without also building an organization that has the capability and the capacity to execute at a high level in the face of extremely rapid growth.

The challenges, risks, and headaches of blitzscaling go beyond the operational; they can take a toll on organizational happiness. "But the thing that keeps these companies together—whether it's PayPal, Google, eBay, Facebook, LinkedIn, or Twitter," Hoffman says, "is the sense of excitement about what's happening and the vision of a great future."

volumes. Defensively, you want to scale faster than your competitors because the first to reach customers may own them, and the advantages of scale may lead you to a winner-takes-most position. And in a global environment, you may not necessarily be aware of who your competition really is.

Are there several dimensions to the idea of scale?

There are three kinds of scale. People naturally focus on two of them: growing your revenues and growing your customer base. And of course, if you don't get those right, then nothing else matters. But very few businesses can succeed on those fronts without also scaling the organization. An organization's size and its ability to execute determine whether it can capture customers and revenue.

We see scale as a series of stages, based on orders of magnitude: A family-scale business can measure its employees in single digits; a tribe in tens; a village in hundreds; a city in thousands. A nation has more than 10,000 employees. These are estimates, not precise guides; a company often remains a family until around 15 employees, a tribe until around 150, and so on.

At each level, the way you run various functions—financing the company, hiring and onboarding employees, marketing the product, and so on—changes significantly. There aren't rules governing this when you're blitzscaling; you use heuristics instead—and by that I mean guidelines that help you make decisions and learn on the fly.

Organizational scale is more about the character of the company than it is an exact employee head count—things don't change drastically at exactly 150 employees. And you're not necessarily scaling each element of the firm at the same time or rate. You're more likely to focus first on customer service and sales than other functions. But even then, you'll have to blitzscale the other parts of the organization. So all along you really do need to be thinking about the company as a whole: How will you allocate your talent, and then how

---

Levels of organizational scale

A glossary

	Number of employees	User scale	Revenue
Family	<10	<100K	<$10M
Tribe	10–100	100K–1M	$10M+
Village	100–1,000	1M–10M	$100M+
City	1,000–10,000	10M–100M	$1B+
Nation	>10,000	>100M	$5B+

will you grow it? How will you hold on to your culture? How will you communicate? How will your competitive landscape shift?

When does a start-up begin to blitzscale?

At the family scale, you're usually raising money and figuring out exactly what your product or service is. You most likely have not launched a product yet.

At the tribe scale, you're just starting to have a real company. It's fairly rare—not unheard of, but rare—for blitzscaling to start at this phase unless you have a runaway hit of a product: PayPal or Instagram, for example. More typically, you've launched some version of the product or service, and you've homed in on your target market. But you're still not certain that the start-up can really scale massively. There's always some level of risk. You may decide not to scale at this stage, because you're not sure you have a product-market fit yet. Or you may decide to move ahead anyway, because you know you absolutely need to, for the offensive and defensive reasons we just talked about.

So the blitzscale process usually starts between the tribe and village scale. By then you've ironed out the product-market fit, you have some data, and you know what the competitive landscape looks like.

This is when the logic of blitzscaling becomes very clear. Once you begin to prove—to yourself and others—that there's an interesting category and a big market opportunity, you attract all kinds of competition. At the low end, other start-ups may be launching their own version of your product or service and trying to achieve scale in the market before you. At the high end, established brands are figuring out how to leverage their own assets to own part or all of your space.

A start-up has two advantages as a first mover going through blitzscale: focus and speed. Established brands tend not to be as fast or as focused. And competing start-ups probably don't have momentum yet (although they may be just as fast and focused).

The canonical example is Groupon, which made it to this middle stage and got hit by massive competition on both the high and the low ends. It wasn't able to both scale fast and build a durable product and thus failed to fully realize a potentially industry-transforming opportunity.

What organizational issues do you run into when blitzscaling?

Blitzscaling is always managerially inefficient—and it burns through a lot of capital quickly. But you have to be willing to take on these inefficiencies in order to scale up. That's the opposite of what large organizations optimize for.

In hiring, for instance, you may need to get as many warm bodies through the door as possible, as quickly as you can—while hiring quality employees and maintaining the company culture. How do you do that? Different companies use different hacks. As part of blitzscaling at Uber, managers would ask a newly hired engineer, "Who are the three best engineers you've worked with in your previous job?" And then they'd send those engineers offer letters. No interview. No reference checking. Just an offer letter. They've had to scale their engineering fast, and that's a key technique that they've deployed.

We faced this issue at PayPal. In early 2000, payment transaction volume was growing at a compounding rate of 2% to 5% per day. That kind of growth put PayPal in a deep hole as far as customer service was concerned. Even though the only place we listed our contact information was in the Palo Alto phone directory, angry customers were tracking down our main number and dialing extensions at random. Twenty-four hours a day, you could pick up literally any phone and talk to an angry customer. So we turned off all our ringers and used our cell phones. But that wasn't a solution. We knew we needed to build a customer service capacity—fast.

But that's very difficult to do in Silicon Valley. So we decided to scale up in Omaha. This was during the first dot-com boom, so we convinced the governor of Nebraska that he wanted a piece of the internet revolution. He and the mayor held press conferences about how PayPal was going to open a customer service office, prompting a flood of job applicants. For four weekends straight, we flew out about 20% of the company to interview them. People showed up with their résumés, and we'd put them in a room and do group

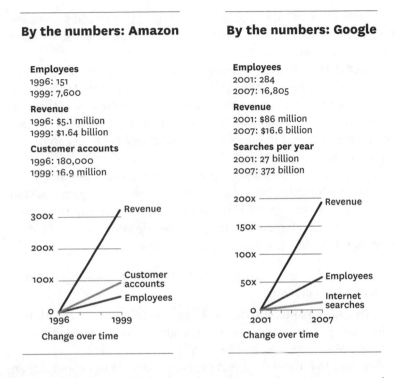

By the numbers: Amazon

Employees
1996: 151
1999: 7,600

Revenue
1996: $5.1 million
1999: $1.64 billion

Customer accounts
1996: 180,000
1999: 16.9 million

By the numbers: Google

Employees
2001: 284
2007: 16,805

Revenue
2001: $86 million
2007: $16.6 billion

Searches per year
2001: 27 billion
2007: 372 billion

interviews. Within six weeks, we had 100 active customer-service people fielding e-mails.

It's now a classic technique for internet companies to offer e-mail and web-based customer service only. But we had to figure out how to hack our customer service challenge at a very fast pace. There was no playbook to tell us what to do. There still isn't.

If there are no rules, how do you come up with your approach?

Sometimes freedom from normal rules is what gives you competitive advantage. For example, if we had understood how pernicious credit card fraud and chargebacks were in the early days at PayPal, I'm not sure we would have believed that such a service could be successful. We didn't realize how staggering the losses could be.

All the banking people knew the rules—you had to protect against fraud first. That prevented them from trying anything that looked remotely like PayPal. Our ignorance allowed us to build something fast, but then of course we had to fix it on the run, because we were already in the minefield.

Most critics thought we were losing so much money in 2000 because of our customer acquisition bonuses. But that wasn't the case. The industry's average customer-acquisition cost through advertising was around $40. So when we gave customers who recommended a friend 10 bucks and gave the new customer 10 bucks, we were cutting costs in half.

Why depend on heuristics rather than rules? Because you're looking for an edge that distinguishes you from other competitors, who are following conventional wisdom. That's not to say that there aren't rules. Don't allow anyone to embezzle your money. That's a rule. But it doesn't give anyone a competitive edge.

It sounds as if your choice of heuristics can lead to radically different organizational outcomes.

Yes. One of the differentiators between Google and Microsoft, two blitzscaling companies, was that Google wanted to stay very flat, whereas Microsoft built up a lot of hierarchy.

You had to have eight direct reports at Google to be a manager, but there was no upper limit. People had 10, 15, 20, even 100 direct reports to minimize middle management. It would likely have been more managerially efficient to give someone no more than eight people. However, Google chose a flat organization that sacrificed that kind of efficiency to achieve an extreme focus on technology development. Microsoft, on the other hand, followed a more classical and hierarchical approach.

That reminds me of Google's decision to hire only people with very high GPAs from elite universities. As a heuristic, there's obviously collateral damage—there are many smart people you're not allowed to hire—but it makes sense if your goal is to hire a large number of smart generalists quickly.

That created a lot of frustration. "I can't hire my friend who doesn't have that qualification, but I know that he's really good." And the company says, "Yeah, sorry. That's the way we execute as we blitz-scale. We need a simple heuristic so that we can focus on what really matters." Another benefit of Google's decision to hire only from elite universities is that it helped create and maintain a coherent culture as the company scaled.

Why is culture so important to blitzscaling?

Because you're growing an organization very fast, you have to make people accountable to each other on a horizontal or peer-to-peer basis, and not just vertically and top-down through the hierarchy.

What other heuristics are important as you go from, say, village to city?

Specialization at all levels becomes more important. You need to understand how to run a large-scale engineering department, for example, and how to deploy a significant amount of capital in marketing. You need dashboards and analytics and metrics for those functions as much as you need them to help you understand customers and the marketplace.

You also need to have much higher reliability; sometimes the inefficiency that you accepted as you blitzscaled through the village stage is no longer tenable at a larger scale. You have to hire people who know how to make sure that your site is never down. And you have to be more careful in your release of engineering product. As a result, you have less adaptability. For example, Facebook famously shifted from a mantra of "Move fast and break things" to "Move fast with stable infrastructure."

You also move from a single-threaded organization to a multi-threaded one, allowing the company to focus on more than one thing at a time. When you're in a tribe, everybody is attuned to one priority. In a village, you're likely to start focusing on the thing that you're going to scale. You're also beginning to think about side experiments—for example, building developer tools, or experimenting with marketing or other paid acquisition. And you're likely adding new functions, like corporate development to consider acquisitions.

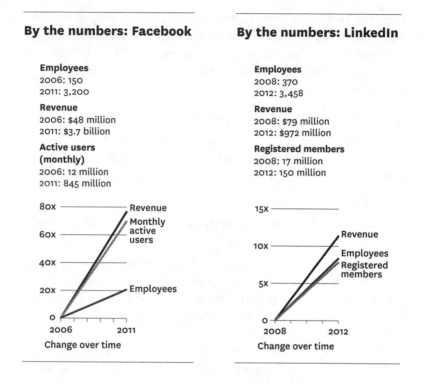

By the numbers: Facebook

Employees
2006: 150
2011: 3,200

Revenue
2006: $48 million
2011: $3.7 billion

Active users (monthly)
2006: 12 million
2011: 845 million

80x — Revenue
Monthly active users
60x —
40x —
20x — Employees
0
2006   2011
Change over time

By the numbers: LinkedIn

Employees
2008: 370
2012: 3,458

Revenue
2008: $79 million
2012: $972 million

Registered members
2008: 17 million
2012: 150 million

15x —
Revenue
10x —
Employees
Registered members
5x —
0
2008   2012
Change over time

All of this rolls up to your macro goal of succeeding as a company, but as you move from village to city, functions are beginning to be differentiated; you're really multi-threading.

Companies at the city scale usually have more than one main product. They may have one central revenue stream, such as Google's AdWords or Microsoft Office, but several different products. They've built an architecture that determines how the products relate to each other. And each product can be multi-threaded as well.

Most Silicon Valley firms go global as they move from village to city, but some are global from Day One. At LinkedIn, we launched with 15 countries on our drop-down list. By the second day, we were getting e-mails from people whose countries were not on the list. It was an interesting geographic lesson for me, because I wasn't aware that the Faroe Islands was a country until we got a complaint. So I went and read a little history and said, OK, add it to the list. It's real.

Do different pockets of the company use different playbooks?

Yes. For example, Google developed two device operating systems simultaneously: Android and Chrome. When Google acquired Andy Rubin and his start-up, Android Inc., Andy was set up as an entrepreneur within Google, focused on this experiment, and accountable to Larry Page. From Google's corporate resources perspective, it was a matter of asking Andy what he needed to make the project work.

Andy wanted Android to stay cohesive and focused. So for example, only Android employees' badges would grant access to the Android office; general Google employees couldn't get in. The Android team didn't run its software through Google's standard code review process. Andy also wanted to be able to cut different deals with mobile operators—whatever it took to get his project off the ground—without a cross-check.

In a completely different initiative, Chrome was developed in C++ (Android was developed in Java) and focused on laptops and browsers, rather than phones. Google could have handled that differently, by bundling Android and Chrome into one project, coherently attacking the device OS opportunity. But it chose instead to multi-thread, hiring the best person for the project, giving him the tools to get the job done, and letting him run a completely separate project and develop his own playbook.

One of the questions I've heard you ask is, What can you ignore? And maybe the flip side of that is, At each stage, what first-order problems are you solving?

One of the metaphors that I use for start-ups is, you throw yourself off a cliff and assemble your airplane on the way down. If you don't solve the right problem at the right time, that's the end. Mortality puts priorities into sharp focus.

When you're blitzscaling, a whole bunch of things are inevitably broken, and you can't work on them all at once. You have to triage.

You fix the things that will get investors to give you more cash. The lift that capital provides means you have a longer time in the air to get things right. You're unlikely to get your plane to fly on your first capital lift or even your second.

A general principle of management is that if you have team dynamics problems, you fix them right away. But in blitzscaling, you're adding those challenges all the time. And you're moving so fast that today's problems aren't going to be the same as tomorrow's. The operation is always patched together and kind of ugly and held together with duct tape. So maybe you ignore the team's dysfunction for a while.

For example, your engineers might be unhappy. You think, Should we build development tools to help them be more productive? Should we allocate a bunch of our engineers to make that happen? But you know that the size of the team will continue to change radically; any tools you create today are going to be obsolete. So you don't try to solve that problem yet, even though you know that ignoring it will breed organizational unhappiness and that people will be frustrated. In nonblitzscaling circumstances those kinds of issues might be a top priority, but when you're blitzscaling, sometimes you have to just let them burn.

Remember, even if you do solve the problem, it will most likely stay solved only for a short time.

Can you alleviate unhappiness by telling people why you're making certain decisions?

Yes, but only to a limited extent. What really keeps it all together is the perception that you're moving at high speed because you're growing something big, and that you're going to be part of something successful.

Almost every blitzscaling org that I have seen up close has a lot of internal unhappiness. Fuzziness about roles and responsibilities, unhappiness about the lack of a clearly defined sandbox to operate in. "Oh my God, it's chaos, this place is a mess." The thing that keeps these companies together—whether it's PayPal, Google, eBay, Facebook, LinkedIn, or Twitter—is the sense of excitement about what's happening and the vision of a great future. Because I'm part of a team that's doing something big, I'll work through my local unhappiness. Sure, I'd like a tidier sandbox, I'd like to be more efficient, I'd like the organization to be run more smoothly. But I'm willing to let it go because the pain will be worth it.

Originally published In April 2016. Reprint R1604B

Buying Your Way into Entrepreneurship

by Richard S. Ruback and Royce Yudkoff

MANY ASPIRING LEADERS take conventional routes to the top in business: They get on a C-suite track at a large company, climb the ladder to partnership at a consulting or investment firm, or launch their own start-up. But there is another career path that has become increasingly popular in recent years: buying and running an existing operation—or what we call *acquisition entrepreneurship*. A record number of such transactions occurred in the United States during the first three quarters of 2016, according to BizBuySell, an online small-business marketplace.

Every year, we teach a course at Harvard Business School on this kind of entrepreneurship, which dozens of students—and others—pursue. Among them are Tony Bautista, who did stints in investment management and business development before taking the helm of Fail Safe Testing, a company that tests equipment for local fire departments; Greg Ambrosia, who served as a U.S. Army officer before acquiring and leading City Wide Building Services, a commercial property window-cleaning specialist in the Dallas/Fort Worth area; and Jennifer Braus, an engineer-turned-MBA who now owns and runs Systems Design West, which manages billing for ambulances and other emergency service providers near Seattle. (Full disclosure:

We are investors in and directors of all three companies.) Other students of ours have gone into home health care, exotic travel, musical instrument rental, specialized software, and manufacturing.

Whether acquisition entrepreneurship is right for you depends on your preferences and temperament. But most of the individuals we've taught, advised, and tracked have found it to be personally, professionally, and financially rewarding.

Perhaps the biggest benefit is instant impact. Instead of navigating a corporate bureaucracy or toiling away on business plans and prototypes, you're immediately in charge of a living, breathing organization and making decisions that have consequence. That was appealing to Braus. "I'm someone who craves responsibility," she says, "so I didn't really like being a worker bee. I saw where I wanted to go in terms of leadership, and now I'm there."

Another plus is having a more flexible lifestyle than might be possible at a fledgling start-up or a large firm. When you're running a stable operation, you rarely need to work nights and weekends, and as the boss, you set the rules: If you want to leave early for a family or community commitment, you can.

But small-business acquisition and management is not without its challenges. That's why you need to make sure you're suited to it and then approach your search, deal negotiation, and transition to leadership in a systematic way. Through our research on multiple companies and their buyers, we've developed a road map for tackling all of these steps.

Reflection

To succeed at acquisition entrepreneurship, you of course need basic management skills: an understanding of finance, a knack for leading and managing others, and an aptitude for decision making. But you need other attributes, too.

Confidence and persuasive ability are key; the job requires you to reach out and project optimism to people you don't know—business brokers, investors, sellers, and the employees and customers you inherit. City Wide's Ambrosia says he felt instantly comfortable

Idea in Brief

An increasingly popular route to success as a small business owner is "acquisition entrepreneurship"—buying and running an existing operation. If you're considering such a path, the authors offer practical advice for each stage of the process.

- **Think it through.** Do you have the right qualities for the job (managerial skills, confidence, persuasiveness, persistence, a thirst for learning, and tolerance for stress)? Are you willing to trade the benefits of working at a large organization for the chance to be in charge?

- **Search diligently and efficiently.** Plan to spend six months to two years—full time—following leads and systematically vetting business prospects. Focus

on companies that are consistently profitable and have annual revenues of $5 million to $15 million. During this phase, you can self-finance or establish a search fund to recruit potential investors.

- **Strike a deal.** When you've settled on a target, do preliminary due diligence to confirm the business's viability and arrive at a fair offer. If the seller accepts, you'll have about 90 days to work with your accountant and attorney on confirmatory due diligence.

- **Transition into leadership.** After the sale closes, your priorities should be building relationships (with employees, customers, and suppliers) and setting up processes to ensure steady cash flow.

with that part of the role, thanks to his military experience, which involved leading different groups of soldiers (including many who were older than he was) on combat missions in Afghanistan.

Persistence—what Bautista describes as "thick skin and grit"—is crucial, too. When seeking a business to buy, you might find a great prospect, reach agreement with the owner on price and terms, and work for months to close the deal—only to have it fall apart at the last minute. You need the fortitude to bounce back. And once you're an owner, it will be up to you to drive the company forward and ensure that it recovers from setbacks.

Additionally, and perhaps most importantly, you should be an enthusiastic learner. Throughout your search, you'll have to quickly get up to speed on unfamiliar industries, sectors, and companies.

When you find an interesting target, you'll need to become knowledgeable about the business. And as an owner and CEO, you must be able to develop expertise across functional areas, stay curious, and recognize that you can and should grow into the job. "Nothing can prepare you for owning a company other than owning a company," Bautista comments. "No day is boring."

It's also important to reflect on the trade-offs that all entrepreneurs make in choosing to go out on their own: Do you value what you'll gain more than what you'll lose? For example, you'll have professional independence and the ability to make unilateral decisions, but that comes with a great deal more pressure. You'll be giving up the comfort of working in a larger, more structured organization where you have greater access to capital, a better-known brand in which to take pride, and the support of peers, bosses, and functional groups such as HR and R&D. Yes, your pay will be directly linked to your performance, with every positive move you and your employees make benefiting you and your investors. But there is a negative flip side: Inevitable mistakes and down cycles will hit you harder than they would if you were a cog in a corporate machine.

"You and the company become one, so you take both the good and the bad," Bautista says. Ambrosia describes the job as "exhilarating" but also "stressful"—sometimes even more so than his time in the army. Leading troops, he alternated between periods of extreme challenge and rest, he explains. But in his role as CEO, that "feeling of responsibility to get it right"—for customers, employees, and investors—"doesn't stop."

So carefully consider what you're in for. If, after all this thinking, you determine that you have the skills and the appetite to become a small-business owner, you're ready to begin your search.

The Search

Although would-be entrepreneurs often worry about making mistakes once they take over a business, it's actually much earlier that many falter. According to research by a team at Stanford University, about a quarter of acquisition searches end without a successful purchase. In other cases, people let emotion or a desire for expediency lead them into buying bad businesses (or the wrong ones for them) or overpaying. We've focused on avoiding these outcomes in our work advising former students and in making investments ourselves. Here's what we suggest.

Whether you're working alone or with a partner, you need to commit to searching full-time for six months to two years. This may sound extreme, but an extended period is necessary to raise funds from investors, identify potential acquisition prospects, thoroughly vet the best of them, negotiate with sellers, and, eventually, find one that agrees to sell at a reasonable price. Then it will take at least three more months to perform due diligence and complete the transaction.

Establishing a search fund is the most popular way to raise enough capital for out-of-pocket expenses and your cost of living during this time. The process involves approaching potential backers (wealthy individuals in your network or those in the small-business-acquisition community) and offering them a first look at investing in an eventual acquisition at favorable terms. Bautista, Ambrosia, and Braus all went about their searches this way. Their aim was to acquire not just money but also advisers who could help them through the deal process, since none of them had M&A experience.

An alternative is to self-finance. To make this realistic, you should try to keep expenses down—one of our students spent only $25,000 over his 14-month search, in part because he was able to live with his in-laws—and limit the number of prospects you consider. The advantage of this route is that you can strike a better deal with investors when you raise money at the acquisition stage.

The search begins by sourcing and filtering prospects. We recommend focusing on companies with annual revenues of $5 million to $15 million and annual cash flows of $750,000 to $3 million. In this range, there are high-quality small businesses available for prices low enough that you and your investors can earn an excellent return even if the business grows only slowly. Forget rapidly evolving start-ups and risky turnaround opportunities; you should look for steady (often unglamorous) enterprises that are profitable year after year and likely to remain so—what we call *enduringly profitable*. While these are strong businesses, you can still add a lot of value by applying best management practices that the current owners might not know about or have the energy to pursue.

In a typical search you'll encounter acquisition prospects every day—through referrals from your network or brokers or through your own direct outreach to business owners. These prospects might total in the thousands over a year or two, so you will need to dismiss most of them very quickly. We recommend that you evaluate each using five criteria:

- Is it profitable?

- Is it an established business?

- Are its revenues and cash flows in the desired range?

- Do you have the skills to manage it?

- Does it suit your lifestyle (location, hours, need for travel, and so on)?

If you can answer yes to all of the above, ask two additional questions that take a bit more time to investigate:

- How enduringly profitable is the business?

- Is the owner serious about selling it?

Markers of enduring profitability include a steady, loyal customer base; a strong reputation; deep integration with customers' systems; large switching costs; and few or no competitors. Examine the financials carefully and look for strong margins and low customer churn. (For more details, see our *HBR Guide to Buying a Small Business.*)

Over a 12-month period, Ambrosia considered approximately 7,500 businesses, from a slaughterhouse to a confectionary company. He indicated interest in 26 and received favorable responses from two before he entered into exclusive negotiations with the seller from whom he eventually purchased his company. Bautista looked at hundreds of prospects (often pestering brokers for details on promising ones), created a short list of 15, and visited five or six before settling on his target. As for Braus, she acknowledges that she "came across a lot of garbage" before finding one candidate that "stood out."

If a business owner has engaged a broker, it's a good sign that he or she is ready to sell. But it's not uncommon for people to back out at the last minute. To counter this risk, spend time with potential sellers as early as possible to investigate their motives. Are they retiring? Have they had a life change that requires them to give up the business? Are they just testing the waters? Consider their expectations: What price do they want? Are they just looking to turn a big profit— or perhaps get rid of a bad apple? And be sure that you've talked to *all* the owners; someone else with a share may be less interested in selling than the person with whom you've been dealing. Even as you dig more deeply into businesses that make it past your initial filters, you should continue to review new prospects in case your desired deal falls through.

Negotiating a Deal

You may have spent only a day or so on the prospect thus far, but if it's still of interest, you should now devote substantially more time to *preliminary due diligence*: a focused period of rapid learning in preparation for making an offer. This is when you'll test the seller's initial claims and verify the information that has made the business appealing to you. You believe the company has many devoted customers because it reported a low churn rate—but are those customer businesses themselves healthy? You think cash flows are steady— but what did the books look like during the last recession? And how sound are the company's current business practices (regarding quality control, billing, refunds, pay, and benefits)? You're looking for any reason that you might *not* want to acquire this business.

Use the company's historical financial data to project future earnings and your return on investment. These calculations will allow you to value the firm as accurately as possible—and thus to arrive at an offer price, typically between three and five times the current EBITDA. Visit banks and approach your investor network to raise money for the acquisition. You should be prepared to provide information about the business and its industry, details on the due diligence that you've done, your financial projections, and the deal terms that you are proposing.

Especially if you're competing against other interested parties, this is also the time to persuade the seller that *you* are the right buyer. Bautista was up against private equity funds willing to spend more money on Fail Safe than he and his investors were, but he won out by emphasizing that he really cared about the business and would continue the owner's legacy.

If your offer is accepted—or accepted after negotiations—you'll enter a period of *confirmatory due diligence* in which the company's records will be fully open to you. You will typically have around 90 days to work with your accountant and attorney to check for any inconsistencies and red flags. (It's a good idea to wait until this stage before bringing in these outside professionals so that you don't have to pay them should the deal fail, as is more likely earlier in the process.) This can be an extremely nerve-racking time for both the buyer and the seller, so it's important to be patient and calm.

"I was always trying to communicate that progress was being made," Ambrosia recalls. Braus's seller threatened to back out when the company signed a big new client 10 days before their deal was scheduled to close, but she and her investors pulled the seller back by renegotiating some of the terms. "Living with the uncertainty during that period was a difficult thing to do," she says, "but we weren't willing to lose the business over it."

Transitioning into Leadership

After closing the sale, you should focus on four tasks: introducing yourself to all your managers and employees, meeting with external stakeholders, communicating the transition plan to everyone, and taking control of your cash flow.

As you meet your new colleagues, reassure them that they won't see any immediate changes. Instead, share your overarching goals for the company—for example, excellent customer service, commitment to quality, a satisfying work environment—and encourage people to stay focused on their work. Also give them an opportunity to ask you questions, but don't feel as if you should have definitive answers for everything: "I want to learn more about that issue before I make a decision" is a fine response.

On the day Ambrosia announced his purchase of City Wide, he stood up in front of his 50 or so employees and delivered a three-part message: He'd bought the business because it was already a great one, everyone's job was secure, and he looked forward to learning from them. He then met with his managers, laying out his expectations for them (mainly codifying existing responsibilities) and telling them what to expect from him. He also made sure to "lead from the front" in his first few weeks—rolling up his sleeves to clean windows with both day and night crews.

You'll need to take the same proactive approach with customers, suppliers, and your new community. All these stakeholders will want to meet the new boss, and many will offer useful ideas about how to improve your offerings. Two other acquisition entrepreneurs we know made a point of visiting every major customer as soon as they could; they told us that all their new product and service ideas in the subsequent months came out of those early meetings.

If you have a management transition arrangement with the former owner, be clear with both employees and customers about how it will work. Explain how decisions are now going to be made and whom to approach with certain types of questions or requests.

Along with relationships, cash flow should be a top priority. The most common trouble for small firms under new owners is running out of cash; after all, they are likely to have acquisition debt to service.

So set up a process whereby you approve all payments before they go out, and review your accounts-receivable balances at least weekly. You should also implement a 90-day rolling cash-flow forecast.

The weeks after closing will be exciting, busy, and filled with learning. You'll be pulled in more directions than even an extended business day can accommodate. "It's a shock to everyone," Bautista explains. "You're afraid all your employees are going to quit, and they're all worried you're going to fire them. And you're responsible for everything right away. I remember thinking 'I'm a 28-year-old now running a 50-person company.'"

Ambrosia and Braus also admit to unexpected early challenges. In the first few months of their tenures, both senior and junior employees left, voluntarily and not, in part because the new owners were bringing more discipline and accountability to their companies. Bautista says he had to drop a few longtime customers that were not actually profitable, and the company experienced a payroll snafu that upset both him and his staff.

But these types of growing pains are inevitable. If you have approached the acquisition process thoughtfully and begun to apply good management, things will soon settle down. And then you'll be able to focus on growing your small business into a successful medium-sized—or even large—one.

Originally published in January–February 2017. Reprint R1701M

The Founder's Dilemma

by Noam Wasserman

EVERY WOULD-BE ENTREPRENEUR wants to be a Bill Gates, a Phil Knight, or an Anita Roddick, each of whom founded a large company and led it for many years. However, successful CEO-cum-founders are a very rare breed. When I analyzed 212 American start-ups that sprang up in the late 1990s and early 2000s, I discovered that most founders surrendered management control long before their companies went public. By the time the ventures were three years old, 50% of founders were no longer the CEO; in year four, only 40% were still in the corner office; and fewer than 25% led their companies' initial public offerings. Other researchers have subsequently found similar trends in various industries and in other time periods. We remember the handful of founder-CEOs in corporate America, but they're the exceptions to the rule.

Founders don't let go easily, though. Four out of five entrepreneurs, my research shows, are forced to step down from the CEO's post. Most are shocked when investors insist that they relinquish control, and they're pushed out of office in ways they don't like and well before they want to abdicate. The change in leadership can be particularly damaging when employees loyal to the founder oppose it. In fact, the manner in which founders tackle their first leadership transition often makes or breaks young enterprises.

The transitions take place relatively smoothly if, at the outset, founders are honest about their motives for getting into business.

Isn't that obvious, you may ask. Don't people start a business to make pots of money? They do. However, a 2000 paper in the *Journal of Political Economy* and another two years later in the *American Economic Review* showed that entrepreneurs as a class make only as much money as they could have if they had been employees. In fact, entrepreneurs make less, if you account for the higher risk. What's more, in my experience, founders often make decisions that conflict with the wealth-maximization principle. As I studied the choices before entrepreneurs, I noticed that some options had the potential for generating higher financial gains but others, which founders often chose, conflicted with the desire for money.

The reason isn't hard to fathom: There is, of course, another factor motivating entrepreneurs along with the desire to become wealthy: the drive to create and lead an organization. The surprising thing is that trying to maximize one imperils achievement of the other. Entrepreneurs face a choice, at every step, between making money and managing their ventures. Those who don't figure out which is more important to them often end up neither wealthy nor powerful.

The trade-off entrepreneurs make

Founders' choices are straightforward: Do they want to be rich or king? Few have been both.

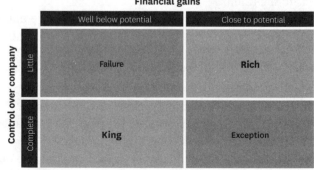

Idea in Brief

Why do people start businesses? For the money and the chance to control their own companies, certainly. But new research from Harvard Business School professor Wasserman shows that those goals are largely incompatible.

The author's studies indicate that a founder who gives up more equity to attract cofounders, new hires, and investors builds a more valuable company than one who parts with less equity. More often than not, however, those superior returns come from replacing the founder with a professional CEO more experienced with the needs of a growing company. This fundamental tension requires founders to make "rich" versus "king" trade-offs to maximize either their wealth or their control over the company.

Founders seeking to remain in control (as John Gabbert of the furniture retailer Room & Board has done) would do well to restrict themselves to businesses where large amounts of capital aren't required and where they already have the skills and contacts they need. They may also want to wait until late in their careers, after they have developed broader management skills, before setting up shop. Entrepreneurs who focus on wealth, such as Jim Triandiflou, who founded Ockham Technologies, can make the leap sooner because they won't mind taking money from investors or depending on executives to manage their ventures. Such founders will often bring in new CEOs themselves and be more likely to work with their boards to develop new, post-succession roles for themselves.

Choosing between money and power allows entrepreneurs to come to grips with what success means to them. Founders who want to manage empires will not believe they are successes if they lose control, even if they end up rich. Conversely, founders who understand that their goal is to amass wealth will not view themselves as failures when they step down from the top job.

Inside the Founder's Mind

Founders are usually convinced that only they can lead their start-ups to success. "I'm the one with the vision and the desire to build a great company. I have to be the one running it," several entrepreneurs have told me. There's a great deal of truth to that view. At the start, the enterprise is only an idea in the mind of its founder, who possesses all the insights about the opportunity; about the innovative product, service, or business model that will capitalize on that opportunity; and about who the potential customers are. The founder hires people to build the business according to that vision and develops close relationships with those first employees. The founder creates the organizational culture, which is an extension of his or her style, personality, and preferences. From the get-go, employees, customers, and business partners identify start-ups with their founders, who take great pride in their founder-cum-CEO status.

New ventures are usually labors of love for entrepreneurs, and they become emotionally attached to them, referring to the business as "my baby" and using similar parenting language without even noticing. Their attachment is evident in the relatively low salaries they pay themselves. My study of compensation in 528 new ventures set up between 1996 and 2002 showed that 51% of entrepreneurs made the same money as—or made less than—at least one person who reported to them. Even though they had comparable backgrounds, they received 20% less in cash compensation than nonfounders who performed similar roles. That was so even after taking into account the value of the equity each person held.

Many entrepreneurs are overconfident about their prospects and naive about the problems they will face. For instance, in 1988, Purdue University strategy scholar Arnold Cooper and two colleagues asked 3,000 entrepreneurs two simple questions: "What are the odds of your business succeeding?" and "What are the odds of any business like yours succeeding?" Founders claimed that there was an 81% chance, on average, that they would succeed but only a 59% probability of success for other ventures like their own. In fact, 80% of the respondents pegged their chances of success at at least 70%—and one in three claimed their likelihood of success was 100%. Founders' attachment, overconfidence, and naïveté may be necessary to get new ventures up and running, but these emotions later create problems.

Growing Pains

Founders eventually realize that their financial resources, ability to inspire people, and passion aren't enough to enable their ventures to capitalize fully on the opportunities before them. They invite family members and friends, angel investors, or venture capital firms to invest in their companies. In doing so, they pay a heavy price: They often have to give up total control over the enterprise. Angel investors may allow entrepreneurs to retain control to a greater degree than venture capital firms do, but in both cases, outside directors will join the company's board.

Once the founder is no longer in control of the board, his or her job as CEO is at risk. The board's task is straight-forward if the founder underperforms as CEO, although even when founders are floundering, boards can have a hard time persuading them to put their "babies" up for adoption. But, paradoxically, the need for a change at the top becomes even greater when a founder has delivered results. Let me explain why.

The first major task in any new venture is the development of its product or service. Many founders believe that if they've successfully led the development of the organization's first new offering, that's ample proof of their management prowess. They think investors should have no cause for complaint and should continue to back their leadership. "Since I've gotten us to the stage where the product is ready, that should tell them that I can lead this company" is a common refrain.

Their success makes it harder for founders to realize that when they celebrate the shipping of the first products, they're marking the end of an era. At that point, leaders face a different set of business challenges. The founder has to build a company capable of marketing and selling large volumes of the product and of providing customers with after-sales service. The venture's finances become more complex, and the CEO needs to depend on finance executives and accountants. The organization has to become more structured, and the CEO has to create formal processes, develop specialized roles, and, yes, institute a managerial hierarchy. The dramatic broadening of the skills that the CEO needs at this stage stretches most founders' abilities beyond their limits.

A technology-oriented founder-CEO, for instance, may be the best person to lead a start-up during its early days, but as the company grows, it will need someone with different skills. Indeed, in analyzing the boards of 450 privately held ventures, I found that outside investors control the board more often where the CEO is a founder, where the CEO has a background in science or technology rather than in marketing or sales, and where the CEO has on average 13 years of experience.

Thus, the faster that founder-CEOs lead their companies to the point where they need outside funds and new management skills, the quicker they will lose management control. Success makes founders less qualified to lead the company and changes the power structure so they are more vulnerable. "Congrats, you're a success! Sorry, you're fired," is the implicit message that many investors have to send founder-CEOs.

Investors wield the most influence over entrepreneurs just before they invest in their companies, often using that moment to force founders to step down. A recent report in *Private Equity Week* pithily captures this dynamic: "Seven Networks Inc., a Redwood City, Calif.-based mobile email company, has raised $42 million in new venture capital funding. . . . In other Seven news, the company named former Onebox.com CEO Russ Bott as its new CEO."

The founder's moment of truth sometimes comes quickly. One Silicon Valley–based venture capital firm, for instance, insists on owning at least 50% of any start-up after the first round of financing. Other investors, to reduce their risk, dole money out in stages, and each round alters the board's composition, gradually threatening the entrepreneur's control over the company. Then it usually takes two or three rounds of financing before outsiders acquire more than 50% of a venture's equity. In such cases, investors allow founder-CEOs to lead their enterprises longer, since the founder will have to come back for more capital, but at some point outsiders will gain control of the board.

Whether gradual or sudden, the transition is often stormy. In 2001, for instance, when a California-based internet telephony company finished developing the first generation of its system, an outside investor pushed for the appointment of a new CEO. He felt the company needed an executive experienced at managing the other executives who oversaw the firm's existing functions, had deeper knowledge of the functions the venture would have to create, and had experience in instituting new processes to knit together the company's activities. The founder refused to accept the need for a change, and it took five pressure-filled months of persuasion before he would step down.

He's not the only one to have fought the inevitable; four out of five founder-CEOs I studied resisted the idea, too. If the need for change is clear to the board, why isn't it clear to the founder? Because the founder's emotional strengths become liabilities at this stage. Used to being the heart and soul of their ventures, founders find it hard to accept lesser roles, and their resistance triggers traumatic leadership transitions within young companies.

Time to Choose

As start-ups grow, entrepreneurs face a dilemma—one that many aren't aware of, initially. On the one hand, they have to raise resources in order to capitalize on the opportunities before them. If they choose the right investors, their financial gains will soar. My research shows that a founder who gives up more equity to attract cofounders, nonfounding hires, and investors builds a more valuable company than one who parts with less equity. The founder ends up with a more valuable slice, too. On the other hand, in order to attract investors and executives, entrepreneurs have to give up control over most decision making.

This fundamental tension yields "rich" versus "king" trade-offs. The "rich" options enable the company to become more valuable but sideline the founder by taking away the CEO position and control over major decisions. The "king" choices allow the founder to retain control of decision making by staying CEO and maintaining control over the board—but often only by building a less valuable company. For founders, a "rich" choice isn't necessarily better than a "king" choice, or vice versa; what matters is how well each decision fits with their reason for starting the company.

Consider, for example, Ockham Technologies' cofounder and CEO Jim Triandiflou, who realized in 2000 that he would have to attract investors to stay in business. Soon, he had several suitors

Keeping Founders on Board

WHAT DO BOARDS DO WITH FOUNDERS after asking them to step down as CEO? Ideally, a board should keep the founder involved in some way, often as a board member, and use his or her relationships and knowledge to help the new CEO succeed. As one investor stated, "You can replace an executive, but you can't replace a founder."

Many times, keeping the founder on board is easier said than done. Founders can act, sometimes unconsciously, as negative forces. They can resist the changes suggested by new CEOs and encourage their loyalists to leave. Some boards and CEOs try to manage those risks by taking half-measures, relegating the founder to a cosmetic role, but that can backfire. For instance, at Wily Technology, Lew Cirne agreed to become chief technology officer after giving up the CEO's post; later he saw that not a single person reported to him. His successor also wanted Cirne to give up his position as board chairman. These moves increased Cirne's unhappiness.

In my study of succession in technology start-ups, I found that 37% of founder-CEOs left their companies when a professional CEO came in, 23% took a position below the CEO, and 40% moved into the chairman's role. Another study of high-growth firms reported that, of the founder-CEOs who were replaced, around 25% left their companies while 50% remained on the board of directors for the next five years.

wooing him, including an inexperienced angel investor and a well-known venture capital firm. The angel investor's offer would have left Triandiflou in control of the board: Joining him on it would be only his cofounder and the angel investor himself. If he accepted the other offer, though, he would control just two of five seats on the board. Triandiflou felt that Ockham would grow bigger if he roped in the venture capital firm rather than the angel investor. After much soul-searching, he decided to take a risk, and he sold an equity stake to the venture firm. He gave up board control, but in return he gained resources and expertise that helped increase Ockham's value manifold.

Similarly, at Wily Technology, a Silicon Valley enterprise software company, founder Lew Cirne gave up control of the board and the company in exchange for financial backing from Greylock Partners and other venture capital firms. As a result, CA bought Wily two

Boards can sometimes help founders find new roles. When a founder has an affinity for a particular functional area, such as engineering, the board can offer him or her the luxury of focusing on that area and letting the new CEO "take on all the things you don't like to do." That approach helps founders gain an appreciation for the new CEO's abilities. The more concrete value the new CEO adds, the easier it will be for the founder to accept the transition. What's more, the less similar the new CEO is to the founder—if the new CEO is 10 years older, for instance—the easier it is for the founder to accept the change.

Founders who want to be CEO for a longer time in their next venture need to learn new skills. Accordingly, boards can encourage founders to take on new roles in their companies that will enable them to do so. If they do, founders may even become accomplished enough to regain control. For example, in 1998, when E Ink's board appointed a new CEO, cofounder Russ Wilcox identified skills he needed to strengthen. He therefore rotated through roles in finance, product marketing, sales, and even R&D to fill the gaps in his skill set. In 2004, when the board launched a search for the company's next CEO, it couldn't find anyone more qualified for the job than Wilcox himself and made him CEO—a position he has held ever since.

years later for far more money than it would have if Cirne had tried to go it alone.

On the other side of the coin are founders who bootstrap their ventures in order to remain in control. For instance, John Gabbert, the founder of Room & Board, is a successful Minneapolis-based furniture retailer. Having set up nine stores, he has repeatedly rejected offers of funding that would enable the company to grow faster, fearing that would lead him to lose control. As he told *BusinessWeek* in October 2007, "The trade-offs are just too great." Gabbert is clearly willing to live with the choices he has made as long as he can run the company himself.

Most founder-CEOs start out by wanting both wealth and power. However, once they grasp that they'll probably have to maximize one or the other, they will be in a position to figure out which is more important to them. Their past decisions regarding cofounders, hires, and investors will usually tell them which they truly favor. Once they know, they will find it easier to tackle transitions.

Founders who understand that they are motivated more by wealth than by control will themselves bring in new CEOs. For example, at one health care–focused internet venture based in California, the founder-CEO held a series of discussions with potential investors, which helped him uncover his own motivations. He eventually told the investors that he wanted to "do as well as I can from an equity perspective . . . [and do] what will be required for the company to be successful in the long run." Once he had articulated that goal, he started playing an active role in the search for a new CEO. Such founders are also likely to work with their boards to develop post-succession roles for themselves.

By contrast, founders who understand that they are motivated by control are more prone to making decisions that enable them to lead the business at the expense of increasing its value. They are more likely to remain sole founders, to use their own capital instead of taking money from investors, to resist deals that affect their management control, and to attract executives who will not threaten their desire to run the company. For instance, in 2002, the founder-CEO of a Boston-based information technology venture wanted to raise $5 million in a first round of financing. During negotiations with potential investors, he realized that all of them would insist on bringing in a professional CEO. Saying that he "was not going to hand the company over to someone else," the entrepreneur decided to raise only $2 million, and he remained CEO for the next two years.

One factor affecting the founder's choices is the perception of a venture's potential. Founders often make different decisions when they believe their start-ups have the potential to grow into extremely valuable companies than when they believe their ventures won't be that valuable. For instance, serial entrepreneur Evan Williams built Pyra Labs, the company that coined the term "blogger" and started the Blogger.com site, without the help of outside investors and eventually sold it to Google in 2003. By contrast, two years later, for his next venture, the podcasting company Odeo, Williams quickly brought in Charles River Ventures to invest $4 million. Asked why,

Williams told the *Wall Street Journal* in October 2005: "We thought we had the opportunity to do something more substantial [with Odeo]." Having ceded control quickly in an effort to realize the substantial potential of the company, Williams has had a change of heart, buying back the company in 2006 and regaining his kingship.

Some venture capitalists implicitly use the trade-off between money and control to judge whether they should invest in founder-led companies. A few take it to the extreme by refusing to back founders who aren't motivated by money. Others invest in a start-up only when they're confident the founder has the skills to lead it in the long term. Even these firms, though, have to replace as many as a quarter of the founder-CEOs in the companies they fund.

Rich-or-king choices can also crop up in established companies. One of my favorite examples comes from history. In 1917, Henry Royce was pushed to merge Rolls-Royce with Vickers, a large armaments manufacturer, in order to form a stronger British company. In a chapter in *Creating Modern Capitalism,* Peter Botticelli records Royce's reaction: "From a personal point of view, I prefer to be absolute boss over my own department (even if it was extremely small) rather than to be associated with a much larger technical department over which I had only joint control." Royce wanted control—not money.

Heads of not-for-profit organizations must make similar choices. I recently consulted with a successful Virginia-based nonprofit whose founder-CEO had faced two coup attempts. Early on, a hospital executive who felt he was himself more qualified to lead the organization mounted one takeover bid, and some years later, a board member made the other bid when the venture was beginning to attract notice. The founder realized that if he continued to accept money from outside organizations, he would face more attempts to oust him. Now the question he and his family have to think through is whether to take less money from outside funders even though that means the venture will grow less quickly.

Would-be entrepreneurs can also apply the framework to judge the kind of ideas they should pursue. Those desiring control should restrict themselves to businesses where they already have the skills and contacts they need or where large amounts of capital aren't required. They may also want to wait until late in their careers before setting up shop, after they have developed broader skills and accumulated some savings. Founders who want to become wealthy should be open to pursuing ideas that require resources. They can make the leap sooner because they won't mind taking money from investors or depending on executives to manage their ventures.

Choosing between money and power allows entrepreneurs to come to grips with what success means to them. Founders who want to manage empires will not believe they are successes if they lose control, even if they end up rich. Conversely, founders who understand that their goal is to amass wealth will not view themselves as failures when they step down from the top job. Once they realize why they are turning entrepreneur, founders must, as the old Chinese proverb says, "decide on three things at the start: the rules of the game, the stakes, and the quitting time."

Originally published in February 2008. Reprint R0802G

About the Contributors

MARC ANDREESSEN is a cofounder and general partner of the venture capital firm Andreessen Horowitz.

STEVE BLANK is a consulting associate professor at Stanford University and a lecturer and National Science Foundation principal investigator at the University of California at Berkeley and Columbia University. He has participated in eight high-tech start-ups as either a cofounder or an early employee.

TIMOTHY BUTLER is a senior fellow at Harvard Business School and senior adviser to its Career and Professional Development program. He is the author of *Getting Unstuck: A Guide to Discovering Your Next Career Path* (Harvard Business School Press, 2010).

ANDREI HAGIU is an associate professor in the strategy group at Harvard Business School.

REID HOFFMAN is cofounder and Executive Chairman of LinkedIn, the world's largest professional network, and a partner at the Silicon Valley venture capital firm Greylock. He is a coauthor of *The Alliance: Managing Talent in the Networked Age* (Harvard Business Review Press, 2014).

ADI IGNATIUS is Editor in Chief of *Harvard Business Review*.

DIANE MULCAHY, a former venture capitalist, is the director of private equity for the Ewing Marion Kauffman Foundation, an adjunct lecturer in the entrepreneurship division at Babson College, and an Eisenhower Fellow.

SIMON ROTHMAN is a partner at Greylock Partners. He was formerly the head of operations at eBay and founded eBay Motors. He has served as an adviser to a number of start-ups, including Lyft, TaskRabbit, Tango, and Fiverr.

RICHARD S. RUBACK is a professor at Harvard Business School and the coauthor (with Royce Yudkoff) of the *HBR Guide to Buying a Small Business* (Harvard Business Review Press, 2017).

WILLIAM A. SAHLMAN is a Baker Foundation Professor of Business Administration at the Harvard Business School in Boston, Massachusetts. He has been closely connected with more than 50 entrepreneurial ventures as an adviser, investor, or director. He teaches a second-year course at the Harvard Business School called "Entrepreneurial Finance," for which he has developed more than 100 cases and notes.

TIM SULLIVAN is the Editorial Director of Harvard Business Review Press.

HAMDI ULUKAYA is the founder and CEO of Chobani.

NOAM WASSERMAN is an associate professor at Harvard Business School in Boston. He writes a research blog at founderresearch. blogspot.com.

NORMAN WINARSKY was President of SRI Ventures at SRI International, a world-renowned research institute. He cofounded and led SRI's venture strategy and process, which has resulted in more than sixty ventures worth over $20 billion, including companies such as Nuance, Intuitive Surgical, and Siri.

ROYCE YUDKOFF is a professor at Harvard Business School and the coauthor (with Richard S. Ruback) of the *HBR Guide to Buying a Small Business* (Harvard Business Review Press, 2017).

Index

The most important management ideas all in one place.

We hope you enjoyed this book from *Harvard Business Review*. Now you can get even more with HBR's 10 Must Reads Boxed Set. From books on leadership and strategy to managing yourself and others, this 6-book collection delivers articles on the most essential business topics to help you succeed.

HBR's 10 Must Reads Series

The definitive collection of ideas and best practices on our most sought-after topics from the best minds in business.

- Change Management
- Collaboration
- Communication
- Emotional Intelligence
- Innovation
- Leadership
- Making Smart Decisions

- Managing Across Cultures
- Managing People
- Managing Yourself
- Strategic Marketing
- Strategy
- Teams
- The Essentials

hbr.org/mustreads

Buy for your team, clients, or event.
Visit hbr.org/bulksales for quantity discount rates.